PRODUCER SERVICES IN CITIES OF THE ASIA PACIFIC ECONOMIC REGION: THE CASE OF KUALA LUMPUR, MALAYSIA

PRODUCER SERVICES IN CITIES OF THE ASIA PACIFIC ECONOMIC REGION: THE CASE OF KUALA LUMPUR, MALAYSIA

MORSHIDI SIRAT, ABDUL FATAH CHE HAMAT AND NOORIAH YUSOF

Nova Science Publishers, Inc.
Huntington, New York

Senior Editors: Susan Boriotti and Donna Dennis
Office Manager: Annette Hellinger
Graphics: Wanda Serrano
Information Editor: Tatiana Shohov
Book Production: Cathy DeGregory, Kay Seymour, Jennifer Vogt and Lynette Van Helden
Circulation: Ave Maria Gonzalez, Ron Hedges, Andre Tillman

Library of Congress Cataloging-in-Publication Data
Available upon request.

Includes bibliographical references and index.
ISBN 1-56072-912-0

227 Main Street, Suite 100
Huntington, New York 11743
Tele. 631-424-6682Fax 631-424-4666
e-mail: Novascience@earthlink.net
Web Site: http://www.nexusworld.com/nova

Printed in the United States of America

CONTENTS

LIST OF FIGURES ix

LIST OF TABLES xi

ACKNOWLEDGEMENTS xiii

CHAPTER 1 PRODUCER SERVICES AND CITIES: A PREAMBLE 1

- **1.1. Introduction** 1
- **1.2. Theoretical Context** 2
- **1.3. Conceptual Framework** 6
- **1.4. Aim and Objectives of Study** 7
- **1.5. Services - Definitions and Classifications** 7
- **1.6. Research Design** 11
- **1.7. Survey Methodology** 11
- **1.8. Sample Structure** 12
- **1.9. Secondary Data** 12
- **1.10. Scope and Coverage of Study** 14

CHAPTER 2 SERVICES IN THE MALAYSIAN ECONOMY 15

- **2.1. Introduction** 15
- **2.2. Services and Balance of Payment (BOP) Problems** 15
- **2.3. Growth of Services in the Malaysian Economy - An Overview of Trend and Pattern** 17
- **2.4. Service Activities - Some Salient Features** 23
- **2.5. Producer (professional) Services in Malaysia, 1984-1994 - Some Salient Features** 25
  - 2.5.1 Expanding Professional Services Activities in Malaysia 26
  - 2.5.2 Declining Professional Services Activities in Malaysia 26
- **2.6. Net Income Contribution of Professional Services Activities in Malaysia, 1984-1994** 27
  - 2.6.1 Professional Services Establishments Experiencing Increase in Net Income Contribution 27

2.6.2 Professional Services Establishments Experiencing Decrease in Net Income Contribution 27
2.7. Government Policies and Strategies Towards the Services Sector 28
2.8. Conclusion 29

CHAPTER 3 SERVICES GROWTH IN KUALA LUMPUR 31
3.1. Introduction 31
3.2. Kuala Lumpur - Towards a Service Economy? 31
3.3. Kuala Lumpur - Services Sector Growth 32
3.4. Kuala Lumpur - Net Income Contribution 33
3.5. Professional Services Growth in Kuala Lumpur 35
3.5.1 Declining Professional Services 35
3.5.2 Growing Professional Services 36
3.6. Net Income Contribution from Kuala Lumpur 37
3.7. Location of Producer Services 40
3.8. Discussion and Conclusion 46

CHAPTER 4 SELECTED SERVICE ACTIVITIES IN KUALA LUMPUR: AGGREGATE DATA ANALYSIS 49
4.1. Introduction 49
4.2. Accountancy Establishments: Performance in 1994 50
4.2.1 Principal Statistics and Performance by Legal Status and Ownership, 1994 – Kuala Lumpur 50
4.2.2 Principal Statistics and Performance by Ownership and Revenue Size Group, 1994 – Kuala Lumpur 52
4.2.3 Principal Statistics and Performance by Ownership and Total Employment Size Group, 1994 – Kuala Lumpur 52
4.2.4 Principal Statistics and Performance by Ownership and Fixed Assets Size Group, 1994 – Kuala Lumpur 55
4.3. Advertising Establishments: Performance in 1994 55
4.3.1 Principal Statistics and Performance by Legal Status and Ownership, 1994 55
4.3.2 Principal Statistics and Performance by Ownership and Revenue Size Group. 1994 – Kuala Lumpur 58
4.3.3 Principal Statistics and Performance by Ownership and Total Employment Size Group, 1994 – Kuala Lumpur 58
4.3.4 Principal Statistics and Performance by Ownership and Fixed Assets Size Group, 1994 – Kuala Lumpur 60
4.4 Conclusion 63

CHAPTER 5 PROFILES OF PRODUCER SERVICES ESTABLISHMENTS SURVEYED 65
5.1. Introduction 65
5.2. Surveyed Establishments' Characteristics 65
5.3. Aggregate Performance of the Surveyed Establishments 69

5.4.	**Mobility and Locational Characteristics of Producer Services Establishments**	**69**
5.5.	**Summary**	**71**
CHAPTER 6	TRADE AND EXPORT OF PRODUCER SERVICES	73
6.1.	**Introduction**	**73**
6.2.	**Trade Patterns Among Producer Services Establishments**	**74**
6.3.	**Input Requirements Among Producer Services Establishments**	**76**
6.4.	**Client Profile of Producer Services Establishments**	**79**
6.5.	**Service Delivery**	**81**
6.6.	**Conclusion**	**82**
CHAPTER 7	SERVICE STRATEGY	85
7.1.	**Introduction**	**85**
7.2.	**Competitive Strategies**	**86**
7.3.	**Is Focus the Key Element of Service Strategy?**	**87**
7.4.	**Goals of Service Organization**	**91**
7.5.	**Summary**	**93**
CHAPTER 8	ESTABLISHMENTS' PERCEPTIONS	95
8.1.	**Introduction**	**95**
8.2.	**Reasons for Increasing Demand**	**95**
8.3.	**Competition in the Service Market**	**97**
8.4.	**Concentration of the Service Industry**	**99**
8.5.	**Market Entry Conditions**	**100**
8.6.	**Government's Attitude Towards the Producer Service Industry**	**103**
8.7.	**Export Potentials of the Producer Service Industry**	**104**
8.8.	**Case Studies**	**107**
8.9.	**Case Study 1 (Accountancy firm)**	**108**
8.9.1.	Introduction	108
8.9.2.	Core Activities	108
8.9.3.	Operating Issues	109
8.9.4.	Problems in Importing or Exporting Services	110
8.9.5.	Impact and Influences of Government Regulations	111
8.10.	**Case Study 2 (Advertising firm)**	**112**
8.10.1.	Introduction	112
8.10.2.	Locational Characteristics	112
8.10.3.	Advantage/Disadvantage of Being a Foreign-Based Firm	113
8.10.4.	Firm's Responses to Government Regulations	114
8.10.5.	Firm's Response to the Economic Crisis	115
8.11.	**Case Study 3 (Architecture firm)**	**116**
8.11.1.	Introduction	116
8.11.2.	Firm's Marketing and Positioning Strategy	116
8.11.3.	Potential Exportability of Architectural Services	117
8.11.4.	Government's Role in Promoting Services –	

8.11.3. Potential Exportability of Architectural Services 117
8.11.4. Government's Role in Promoting Services – Firms' Perception and Recommendations 118
8.12. Case Study 4 (Information Technology Firm) 119
8.12.1. Introduction 119
8.12.2. Location Characteristics 119
8.12.3. Operational Problems and Constraints 120
8.12.4. Export Potentials 121
8.12.5. Firm's Perception on Government Roles 122
8.12.6. Recommendations to the Government 122
8.13. Discussion and Conclusion 123

CHAPTER 9 CONCLUSION AND POLICY IMPLICATIONS 127
9.1. Introduction 127
9.2. The role and Contribution of Producer Services 128
9.3. Policy Implications 129
9.4. Academic Contributions 131
9.5. Further Research 132

REFERENCES 133

INDEX 141

LIST OF TABLES

Table 1.0	Producer Services Establishments in Kuala Lumpur: Sample Structure	**13**
Table 2.0	Balance of Payments 1990-2000	**16**
Table 2.1	Malaysia: Contribution of Services Sector, 1960-1995	**18**
Table 2.2	Gross Domestic Product by Industry of Origin, 1985-2000	**19**
Table 2.3	Malaysia: Employment by Sector, 1990-2000 ('000 persons)	**22**
Table 2.4	Loans to Major Sectors by the Banking System, 1990 and 1995	**23**
Table 2.5	Performance of Selected Services Industries in Malaysia, 1984-1992	**24**
Table 4.1	Accountancy establishments in Kuala Lumpur: performance by legal status and ownership, 1994	**51**
Table 4.2	Accountancy establishments in Kuala Lumpur: performance by ownership and revenue size group, 1994	**53**
Table 4.3	Accountancy establishments in Kuala Lumpur: performance by ownership and total employment size group, 1994	**54**
Table 4.4	Accountancy establishments in Kuala Lumpur: performance by ownership and fixed assets size group, 1994.	**56**
Table 4.5	Advertising establishments in Kuala Lumpur: performance by ownership and legal status, 1994.	**57**
Table 4.6	Advertising establishments in Kuala Lumpur: performance by ownership and revenue size group, 1994	**59**
Table 4.7	Advertising establishments in Kuala Lumpur: performance by ownership and total employment size group, 1994	**61**
Table 4.8	Advertising establishments in Kuala Lumpur: performance by ownership and fixed assets size group, 1994	**62**
Table 5.1	Characteristics of Surveyed Producer Services Establishments	**68**

LIST OF FIGURES

Figure 1.1	Research Conceptual Framework	8
Figure 2.1	Services Sector: Annual Growth Rate by Sub-Sectors, 1989-1997	21
Figure 3.1	Spatial Distribution of Service Establishments in Kuala Lumpur, 1998 (Miscellaneous Services)	41
Figure 3.2	Spatial Distribution of Service Establishments in Kuala Lumpur, 1998 (Telecommunication, Real Estate and Accounting Services)	42
Figure 3.3	Spatial Distribution of Service Establishments in Kuala Lumpur, 1998 (Banking, Finance and Accounting Services)	43
Figure 3.4	Spatial Distribution of Service Establishments in Kuala Lumpur, 1998 (Recruitment/Employment and Secretarial/Administrative Services)	44
Figure 3.5	Spatial Distribution of Service Establishments in Kuala Lumpur, 1998 (Legal Services)	45
Figure 5.1	Spatial Distribution of the 92 Surveyed Producer Service Establishments in Kuala Lumpur	67

Talbe 5.2	Recruitment by Category of Workers between 1993 through 1997	**71**
Table 6.1	The Degree of Intensity in Terms of Capital, Labor, Skill and Technology in the Supply of Services	**77**
Table 6.2	Types of Other Goods and Service Inputs Required for Production of Services (Rated As Very Important and Important) – Group 1	**77**
Table 6.3	Types of Other Goods and Service Inputs Required for Production of Services (Rated As Very Important and Important)- Group 2	**78**
Table 6.4	Types of Other Goods and Service Inputs Required for Production of Services (Rated As Very Important and Important)-Group 3	**78**
Table 6.5	Types of Other Goods and Service Inputs Required for Production of Services (Rated As Very Important and Important)-Group 4	**79**
Table 6.6	Major (more than 60 percent of total business) and Minor Clients of Producer Services Establishments	**80**
Table 6.7	Service Delivery Styles	**82**
Table 7.1	Choosing Focus as the Competitive Strategy	**87**
Table 7.2	Reasons for Choosing Focus Strategy	**89**
Table 7.3	Choice of Strategic Actions of Focus Strategy	**90**
Table 7.4	Reasons for Not Choosing Focus Strategy	**90**
Table 7.5	Goals of Service Organizations	**91**
Table 8.1	Reasons for Increasing Demand for Producer Services	**96**
Table 8.2	Are There Too Many Suppliers of Producer Services?	**99**
Table 8.3	Is the Competition in the Producer Service Industry Fair?	**99**
Table 8.4	Instances of Unfair Competition	**100**
Table 8.5	Is the Producer Service Industry Highly Concentrated in Kuala Lumpur?	**102**
Table 8.6	Are There Market Entry Conditions for the Services Provided?	**102**
Table 8.7	Some of the Market Entry Conditions Claimed by Establishments	**102**
Table 8.8	The Government's Attitudes Towards the Service Provided	**104**
Table 8.9	Chance of Exporting Services Outside Malaysia	**105**
Table 8.10	Measures to Encourage the Export of Services to Foreign Markets	**106**

ACKNOWLEDGEMENTS

We wish to thank Kevin O'Connor (Department of Geography & Environmental Science, Monash University, Australia), Tom Hutton (Centre for Human Settlements, University of British Columbia, Canada), Bill Beyers (Department of Geography, University of Seattle, Washington) and Peter Daniels (School of Geography and Service Sector Research Unit, The University of Birmingham, United Kingdom). They gave us the opportunity to participate in their research project entitled "Producer Services in the Asia-Pacific Economic Region". In view of data constraints and other problems we were facing, the research approach and methodology as outlined in their original project research proposal had to be slightly modified for our study on Kuala Lumpur. However, this modification is very minor and a comparative analysis of findings with other members of the project team is still feasible.

We are very grateful to the IRPA Service Sector Panel and the Ministry of Science, Technology and Environment, Malaysia for approving a very generous grant to conduct this study. We also gratefully acknowledge support and encouragement given by the Universiti Sains Malaysia, in particular its Research and Development Section.

Our sincere thanks to Haslina Arshat and Azlin Kamardin for their hard work and skills as Research Officers, to Mr Khalid Awang and Mr Chong Woei Weng for their cartographic skills, second year Geography Major students of academic session 1998/99 for conducting the field interviews, and survey respondents for their time and co-operation.

Morshidi Sirat
Abdul Fatah Che Hamat
Nooriah Yusof
Pulau Pinang, Malaysia
3 October 2000

Chapter 1

PRODUCER SERVICES AND CITIES: A PREAMBLE

1.1. INTRODUCTION

Much attention has been given recently to the role and contribution of producer services in advanced economies. In most of these economies, producer services account for no less than 50 percent of employment in metropolitan areas. Evidently, the increase in the share of producer services in all employment has been well documented for Europe and for North America (see Daniels, 1998: 147). In so far as the Asia Pacific economic region is concerned, there is a similar pattern of growth and development although this is only based on employment in finance, insurance, real estate and business services (Daniels, 1998: 147). Producer services represent one of the key new growth sectors, but in the context of the Asia Pacific economic region empirical work about how producer services are participating in, and shaping, the process of development remains to be undertaken (Daniels, 1998: 156). In the case of many developing countries in the Asia Pacific economic region grouping producer services are heavily represented in urban and metropolitan areas, which are more developed and functionally diverse. However, the role and contribution of producer services in the highest of the urban hierarchy in the developing countries of the region has not been examined adequately. This is because many developing countries have focused their attention and resources on developing the manufacturing sector for it was believed that industrialization and manufacturing industry were the panacea for their socio-economic problems (Mountjoy, 1984). This neglect was partly attributed to the definitional and measurement problems of this sector itself. Since the eighties however there were empirical evidences pointing to the positive contributions of the producer services sector in the context of regional and urban economies (for example see Hansen, 1990). Therefore, to appreciate the strategic importance of producer services in urban areas, the basic characteristics and operation of this sector need to be understood and analyzed. This task becomes the more urgent with globalization process and the increasing competition between cities (for example see Cox, 1995). Another major challenge facing national governments in an era of open international markets is whether to liberalize or to protect service-producing firms (for example see Aharoni,

1997). Either way, the decision to intervene in the markets or to retreat will have serious consequences for the economies of cities and urban areas.

1.2. Theoretical Context

Bryson and Daniels (1998a, 1998b) have successfully assembled some of the most important articles pertaining to various aspects of the role and contributions of service activities to local, regional, national and global economies. These selected 'benchmark' papers, some were published as early as 1939 and the latest being 1997, contributed significantly to our understanding of the rise and growth of the service sector. Some papers in these two volumes deal explicitly on the rising importance of producer services. Based on these edited volumes plus many more recent articles and books on producer services it is possible to identify the various theories and explanations pertaining to the role and contributions of this sector in the economy. This is the basis of the following discussion on the theoretical context of this study.

Four major and interlinked strands of theories within the producer services debate form the main thrust of this research. The first set of theories relate to the various determinants of growth in producer services. The literature have attributed the rapid growth of activities within the producer services category to a number of factors, the majority of which relate to the increasing complexity of both the external environment of the firms and its internal organization (for example see Coffey and Bailly, 1991). Arguably, changes in industrial organization or organizational complexity have increased the need for producer services to facilitate the expansion of business in the market. It is also argued that organizational changes in the production process have also given rise to growth in service labour (for example see Bagchi-Sen and Sen, 1997). Among the many other factors that have attributed to the rapid growth in producer services the one that is of primary importance is the subcontracting of indirect production activities by corporations to independent service firms instead of relying on in-house service departments (see Noyelle and Stanback, 1984). This subcontracting process is referred to in producer services literature as externalization and/or unbundling and it is argued that this phenomenon has grown either due to cost or non-cost considerations (see for example, Beyers and Lindahl, 1996). Beyers and Lindahl have provided an extensive review of pure-cost driven considerations in the externalization of services. Elaborating on this phenomenon, Scott (1988) notes that firms externalize services where external provision is less expensive and this includes the acquisition of input factors such as producer services. Other writers such as O'Farrell, Mofatt, and Hitchens (1993), Perry (1992), Goe (1991, 1990), and Coffey and Bailly (1992, 1991) have also discussed the externalization of producer services among firms and why this measure was adopted by firms.

Apart from the most "pure" form of cost-driven externalization, other "less pure" consideration may also influence firms to outsource for services thus bringing about an increase in the number of producer services providers. For example, firms sought outside services because of a perception that outside provision is cheaper, and this view may or may not be based on an actual comparison cost of internal provision or external purchase (cf. Beyers and Lindahl, 1996). Downsizing and perception that outside provision is less expensive - are what one deemed to be the best indicators of cost-driven externalization (cf. Beyers and Lindahl, 1996).

Apart from the pure and not so pure cost consideration, Beyers and Lindahl (1996) have also identified quasi-cost consideration; and these are factors that in some cases may be interpreted in a transaction cost framework, but in others are more related to issues of strategy, scope, and motivations that are indirectly related to the service user's desire to reduce costs. Briefly, under this category, some of the most important factors are flexible approaches to production, whereby firms turn to outside suppliers of producer services in order to reduce cost of production (see for example, Christopherson and Noyelle, 1992; Coffey, 1992; Hatch, 1987). According to Coffey and Bailly (1992), for example, in the context of flexible production systems utilization of producer services are likely to emerge especially when the need for service inputs constantly changes in terms of mixes, in addition to the sporadic and unpredictable nature of the demands of this type of inputs. It is argued that by acquiring producer services in the market place, firms or producer services clients are able to adapt quickly to changing business circumstance without having to endure internal commitments to staff and capital investments (Beyers and Lindahl, 1996). Hansen (1991) elaborating on the aspect of flexibility argues that flexibility is also considered in relation to three strategic areas within the firms i.e., risk reduction, infrequent demands, core skills concentration (Hansen, 1991). On similar note, Beyers and Lindahl (1996) also agree that it is to be expected that sellers or providers of producer services will have clients seeking their services to reduce risks, cope with infrequent needs and make it possible for the purchasers of producer services to concentrate on skills which are important to the industry and markets served by these firms.

Non-cost considerations have also been viewed as determinants of externalization process among buyers of producer services. These include lack of expertise within client firms, thus the need for outsourcing; buyers'/suppliers' dynamics bringing about evolving relationships between producer service firms and their clients in terms of services offered, and the relative importance of external purchase versus internal provision; growing complexity of national and international business environments, leading to the need for more specialists; and increased government regulations and the development of regulations governing the selling and buying of services in the market place and also trade in goods and services (cf. Beyers and Lindahl, 1996).

A second group of theory that is relevant to the argument here comes from debates relating to export decisions of producer services-producing firms and their impacts on the urban regions (see for example Harrington, 1995; Smith, 1984; Smith and Pulver, 1981). Closely related to this idea of export decisions is the expanding body of literature focusing on trade in producer services (at interurban or intermetropolitan scale) as an engine of urban economic growth (see for example Browne, 1991; Keil and Mack, 1986). Evidently, most of the theoretical exposition concerning export potentials of producer services firms and their impacts on the urban economy are based upon some variations of the classical export base theory. Following this theory, export sales bring income into urban areas, fuelling economic growth through the re-spending of this income within the urban region. But, arguably, not all producer services firms are export-oriented in nature. Ashton and Sternal (1978) argued that maybe only large establishments, or only establishments with out-of-state affiliates, or perhaps only establishments which have a specific employee in charge of marketing are able to engage in export activities. But admittedly, as Noyelle (1987, 1983) correctly argue, until recently manufacturing has been a principal component of the export base, but increasingly, however, producer services is becoming a vital sector in the urban economy because of its income-generating export activities. But, apparently the connection between producer service activities and metropolitan economic growth is a complex and tenuous one (see Persky and Wiewel, 1994).

Through empirical investigation Persky and Wiewel (1994) manage to demonstrate that rapid absolute growth of the service sector as a whole resulted in producer services accounting for considerable increases in the share of employment and economic activity throughout the metropolitan hierarchy. But Persky and Wiewel (1994) caution that while the export of producer services has increasing relevance to metropolitan areas, there are reasons to expect that an increasingly higher percentage of activities within the producer services sector in these areas continue to serve local or regional markets. For while many producer services in metropolitan areas have themselves grown and become more export-oriented, the sum of forces at work have tended to increase the local share of metropolitan activity. Outside of major urban areas however the scope for the expansion and specialization of service functions is said to be generally lower (Marshall and Wood, 1995). Even if growth in producer service activities, such as the 1980s boom in US exports of producer services, have had a strong positive impact upon some US metropolitan economies, it is the central cities that stand out as having both high concentration and specialization contributing significantly to export earning (see Drennan, 1992). Davis and Hutton (1994) have arrived at similar conclusion in the context of metropolitan cities in Canada. For them, export-oriented producer services are overwhelmingly clustered within metropolitan cities, and inter-regional and international service trades are conducted largely by firms, institutions, and facilities concentrated within urban areas. They also argue that, the effects of growth in trade among producer services are not dispersed throughout the nation, but are concentrated in metropolitan areas. Undeniably, several impacts are noticeable in urban areas, in particular the CBD, arising from producer services export activities. These are expansions of the urban export base; significant growth impulses transmitted throughout the urban economy by means of the export base multiplier in higher-order service employment; enhancement of the efficiency of the regional production economy; increased functional specialization of the metropolitan core, and "internationalization" of the CBD (Davis and Hutton, 1994).

Quite related to export activities of urban areas is the fact that the larger the place, the higher the concentration in these export services - the greatest variation being demonstrated by the complex of corporate activities in which the largest places have held an unequivocal advantage (Stanback, Bearse, Noyelle, and Karasek, 1981). Thus, they argued that size and agglomeration economies have been the major determinants of the location of export services.

The study reported in this book is also based on various debates concerning the interurban location of producer service activities. The overwhelming importance of face-to-face contact in both the acquisition of inputs and the delivery of the product to clients results in agglomeration-economies-maximizing and transaction-cost-minimizing in corporate activity complexes traditionally located in the CBD (Coffey, Drolet and Polese, 1996). At the same time, Coffey, Drolet and Polese (1996) have argued that the need to maintain less formal face-to-face contact with colleagues in other establishments also plays a significant role, as does the need for establishments to become integrated into the "contact-rich" and "information-rich" business environment of the CBD. Michalak and Fairbairn (1993), Schwartz (1992), Hutton and Ley (1987), Gad (1985, 1979), Ley (1985), and Code (1983) are among others confirming such assertions. Apart from the influencing effect of the need to have face-to-face contact, other variables such as client type and size of establishment have been found to be equally important (see Gad, 1985, 1979).

In term of interurban mobility, Coffey, Drolet and Polese (1996) have shown that, in the context of Montreal, producer services establishments are more mobile than establishments within the category of finance, insurance and real estate (FIRE). They have shown that the latter are not only less likely to shift their location, but when a move does occur the establishments tend to remain within the same geographic zone.

Based on their Montreal study Coffey, Drolet and Polese were able to demonstrate that high-order service establishments that are located in the CBD tend to have one of the two specific profiles as follows: 1) client-oriented establishments that serve intermediate demands (other establishments) located in the down town corporate activities complex through a series of intensive face-to-face contact linkages; or 2) establishments whose principal function is the administration of an enterprise, and who have chosen the information-rich and contact-intensive environment of the CBD in order to enhance their control over their corporate "empires".

Very recently, with the share of FDI in the service sector exceeding the share of FDI in manufacturing in most industrially advanced and new industrializing countries (UNCTC, 1988), internationalization process of producer services has emerged as an important area for research. This body of ideas forms the fourth basis for this research. The assertion is that internationalization of producer services firms arose out of client-following activities rather than strategies relating to market expansion or market diversification (risk diversification) (Bagchi-Sen and Sen, 1997). Global expansion of service companies - companies engaged in activities such as accounting, advertising and real estate - further invigorated the growth of international businesses in all sectors in the foreign market (fro example see Cox, Clegg and Ietto-Giles, 1993; Dicken, 1992; Kaynak, 1989).

Theorists recognized a number of key elements in explaining the growth of MNCs and these could be grouped into firm specific and ownership-specific advantages, location-specific advantages, and internalization advantages (Bagchi-Sen and Sen, 1997, see also Clegg, 1993). Bagchi-Sen and Sen (1997) have provided a succinct summary of the role of the above-mentioned advantages in influencing international location decisions. These are briefly presented as follows. With respect to firm-specific and ownership-specific advantages, it is argued that in an imperfect market, the monopolistic or oliogopolistic structure of an industry offers special advantages to a few large firms in terms of factors such as patented technology, unpatented secret know-how, large capital requirements, economies of large-scale production, and expertise in differentiating products. It is argued further that these become important to firms when they decide to enter into an unfamiliar foreign market, and arguably could determine their success or failure when competing with local service providers (see also Hymer, 1976; Kindleberger, 1969).

The concept of internalization on the other hand, states that a firm will assume coordinating activities itself by producing in the foreign country when it is a more efficient choice than using the market through exporting or licensing (Rugman, 1981; Buckley and Casson, 1976; Caves, 1971, cited in Bagchi-Sen and Sen, 1997). Dunning (1977), however, noted that firm specific and internationalization advantages do not provide sufficient condition for foreign location of firms. He argued that location-specific factors either at home or in host countries have to be considered in conjunction with the above-mentioned advantages arising from either ownership-specific characteristics or internationalization option. In the final analysis, Dunning (1988) hinted that a configuration of ownership, location, and internationalization (OLI) advantages are pertinent to any internationalization of activities.

In the context of business services, Bagchi-Sen and Sen (1997) have generalized that producer service firms have become more market-seeking rather than client-following. Accounting and advertising service firms, for instance, have a tendency to search for new markets not only in geographical terms but also embracing service diversification. These have resulted in corporate reorganization such as mergers across national boundaries to take advantage of economic integration of regions/nations as well as deregulation and liberalization of national economies especially those emerging ones. Organizational evolution such as the formation of branch companies specializing in one service within a large multinational is also becoming evident.

On the basis of the four partly speculative and partly empirical bodies of theories and explanations in the preceding section, objectives of this research were subsequently formulated and operationalized.

1.3. Conceptual Framework

Having reviewed the pertinent theoretical underpinnings it is now possible to present a conceptual framework for the study of producer services in the urban economic development of the City of Kuala Lumpur, Malaysia (Figure 1.1). In this framework it is hinted that service demands would arise from various economic sectors of the urban economy, in particular from the construction, service and manufacturing sectors. As such, the "industrial model" of producer services development was not adopted for it is argued that the development of the service sector is directly tied to and predominantly dependent upon the resources generated by local manufacturing industry. Instead, the conceptual framework (Figure 1.1) was constructed on the premise that producer services growth may be related to the growing size and complexity of firms in all sectors of the economy in addition to the manufacturing sector (for example see Sassen, 1991).

Admittedly, the use of producer services is deemed necessary for the efficient operation of client establishments, although it remains to be investigated how, why and by whom these services are produced. Producer services procurement among establishments in Kuala Lumpur is expected to generate spatial and non-spatial impacts on the urban economy, and these are indicated in Figure 1.1. Ultimately, since Kuala Lumpur is pivotal to Malaysia's development, and a high concentration of producer services establishments are to be found in this city, the sector's impact on national economic scenario need to be charted out. This is reflected in the 'national economic implications' component of the conceptual framework.

1.4. Aim and Objectives of Study

Against the theoretical propositions regarding the role of producer services in the urban economy and its spatial and non-spatial impacts as noted in the preceding section, section, the aim therefore is to examine present status of, and future prospects for, producer services growth in the City of Kuala Lumpur.

Arising from the above aim, the specific objectives are as follows:

(a) To determine the economic activity-producer services linkages in Kuala Lumpur,
(b) To determine the contribution of producer services in the economic growth of Kuala Lumpur,
(c) To determine the relationships between spatial and temporal variations of producer services growth to key endogenous and exogenous forces such as globalization, the rise of transnational corporations, patterns of foreign direct investment, and the regulatory environment,
(d) To formulate policies and strategies that can influence the rate and change in activities relating to the producer services sub-sector in Kuala Lumpur.

1.5. Services - Definitions and Classifications

There have been many attempts to define 'services' and the task appears to be difficult and elusive (for example see Marshall et al., 1988; Stanback, 1979; Singelmann, 1978; Katouzian, 1970; Fuchs, 1968;). Attempts to define services will become more arduous in the future as a result of technological changes. Daniels (1993) for example has noted quite rightly that new service occupations are being generated as a result of technological development, and he has cited the case of computer and software services or specialized information services that have emerged as a result of significant development in telecommunications.

Figure 1.1 Research Conceptual Framework

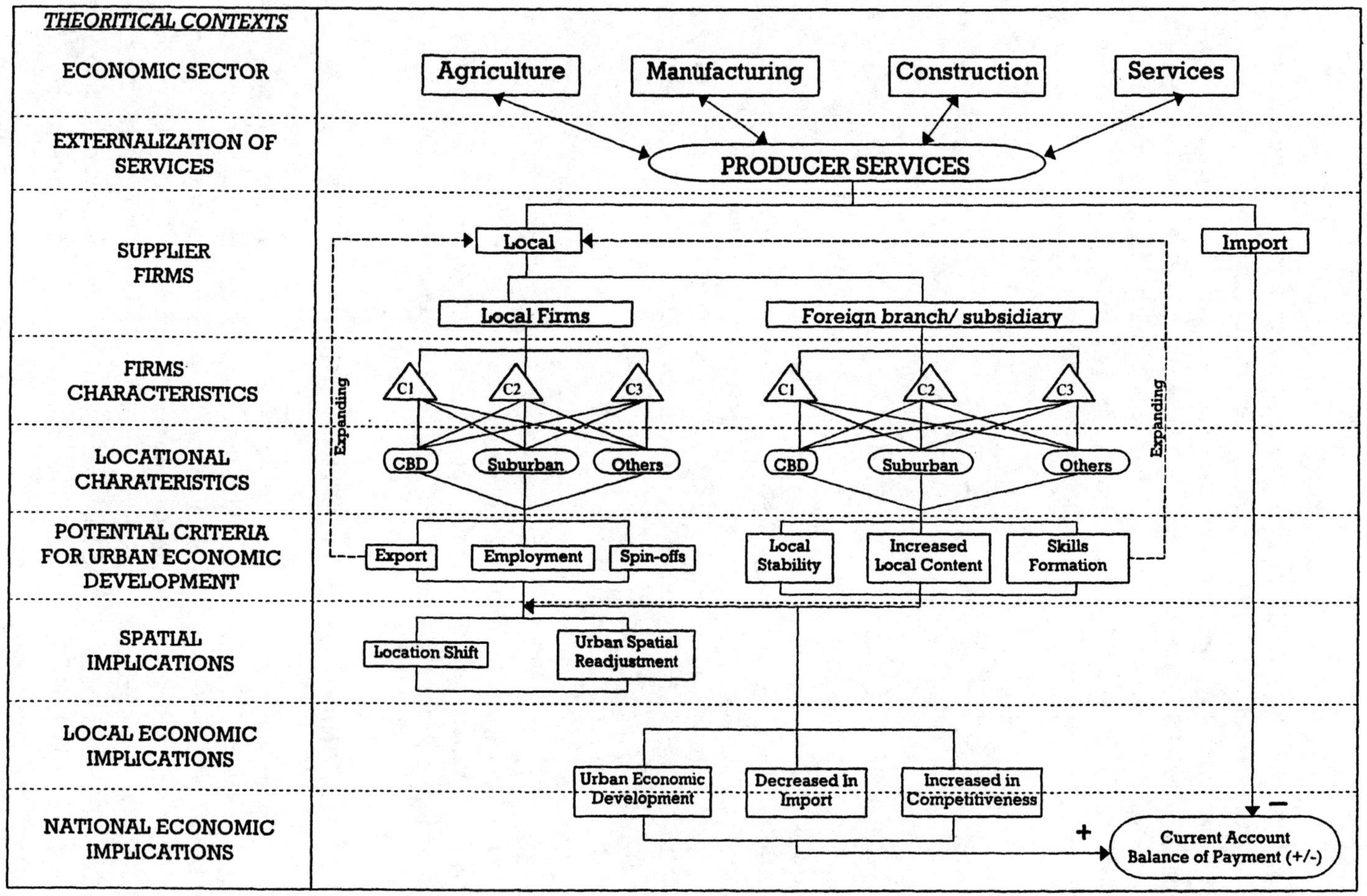

A definition that was espoused by Daniel (1985) - a 'service may be defined as the exchange of a commodity, which may either be marketable or provided by public agencies, and which often does not have a tangible form' - was adopted as a working definition for it meets the aims and objectives as noted earlier. Also, this is a 'neat' definition in comparison to a definition whereby 'services are portrayed as intangible, invisible and perishable, requiring simultaneous production and consumption'. Arguably, Daniels's definition of services follows the economic function-intrinsic value to consumers or providers division, which is arguably very appropriate for policy-oriented analysis. For instance, UNCTAD (1994) is also in favour of a definition that follows the above division primarily for its utility in terms of policy formulation.

Distinction has to be made between consumer/final services and intermediate services within the service sector. Just as there were numerous attempts to define 'services', there are equally numerous attempts to classify 'services'. Katouzian (1970), for example, has suggested a classification scheme based on three main considerations. UNCTAD (1994) has summarized Katouzian's classification as follows. 'New services' category includes those activities that are particularly sensitive to growth in per capita income and leisure time. Examples are entertainment, education and health. 'New' denotes that the mass consumption nature of these activities is a relatively new or recent phenomenon. 'Complementary services' group comprises of activities that are closely linked to the process of urbanization and industrialization (or perhaps, globalization). Activities included in this category are banking, finance, transportation, wholesale and retail trade. 'Old services' group refers to activities, such as domestic and household services, that have been losing economic importance because of substitution effects.

The United States Congress Office of Technology Assessment (1987) has proposed groupings based on the technological contents of service activities. According to their classification, services can be grouped into knowledge-based services and tertiary services. The former comprises of activities such as insurance, professional and technical services, certain banking services, information technology services, advertising, motion pictures, health care, education and some government services). This group is characterized by the relatively high human-capital content and their production method is often customized. The second group - tertiary services - includes leasing, shipping, distribution, franchising, retail trade, travel, some social services, most entertainment and personal services. For this group, human-capital requirement is said to be lower and production method is more standardized. One limitation of this classification is that as production method is frequently changing the demarcation between groups would become blurred over time. However, this is a useful way to look at services if one is interested in analyzing the technological content.

A classification system, which is now widely adopted, is the one based on Browning and Singelmann (1975) and Singelmann (1978). They have suggested that services be grouped into distributive services (e.g. transportation and storage, communication, wholesale and retail trade); producer services (e.g. banking, finance, insurance, real estate, engineering and architectural services, accounting and legal services); social services (e.g. health, education, welfare and religious services, postal services and other governmental services); and personal services (e.g. domestic services, repair services, hotels, restaurants and entertainment). As pointed by Daniels (1993: 5) this classification imposes some order on the diversity of the services industries while at the same time clearly separating them from the transformative industries (manufacturing and construction) industries and extractive activities (agriculture and mining). This classification also separates "goods-oriented" services (distributive and producer services) from "consumption-oriented" services (personal and social services). However, it has to be acknowledged that this classification system is not problem-free either. The classification presupposes that the service sector is somehow exclusive; in practice the boundaries between it and other sectors are becoming blurred as some manufacturers, for example, are also producing services (Daniels, 1993: 5).

Marshall and Wood (1995:35) summarized the whole debate as follows:

> "The definition and classification of services is thus clearly not a neutral, technical matter. It embodies views, some of which are 'historically-based' in the origins of the SIC, obscuring the modern role of services. In examining the construction of a more appropriate framework for the definition and classification of services, a conflict of interpretation has emerged. Those who believe services to be driving new forms of economic production tend to accept to some degree the validity of the categories provided in the SIC, and base their work on their development. Those who argue that service growth represents no more than an elaboration of earlier industrially based developments under capitalism adopt a much narrower definition of what constitutes a service than is provided by the SIC, arguing that many 'service industries' in the SIC are implicated in goods production and circulation."

In the Browning and Singelmann's classification, a distinct service category was identified and this is referred to as 'producer services'. According to Sassen (1991) the initial notion was that these services supported production, whence the name producer services. She correctly highlighted that it has now become evident that these services are also in used in service organizations, both in the public and private sectors. She also observed that since then, the term 'producer services' includes not only services to production firms narrowly defined but also those to all other types of organizations. In fact, much earlier Greenfield (1966) has suggested some differentiating traits for this group of services: 'producer services' are services produced for organizations, whether private sector firms or governmental entities, rather than for final consumers. In other words, 'producer services' are intermediate outputs (Greenfield, 1966).

From a geographical point of view, most studies on 'producer services' generally assume differences in the locational needs and tendencies of consumer-producer service establishments (see for example Daniels, 1985). Consumer services are assumed to be locationally tied to the center of a consumer market of adequate size. Producer services, on the other hand, have the tendency to export from smaller places to larger centers, and from centers outside their usual hinterland (for example see Michalak and Fairbairn, 1988; Beyers and Alvine, 1985).

In this research, the classification system as proposed by Browning and Singelmann was adopted as the working classification of services. This SIC-based framework provides consistent definitions and classifications of services, which is also the basis for much of the official statistics in Malaysia (see for example Sieh, 1992). However, "one problem with operationalizing the producer services sector as a subset of SIC categories is that firms and/or establishments grouped under such industry categories as banking, insurance, real estate and legal services may have mixed producer and consumer markets" (Browning and Singelmann, 1978; Goe, 1990; Sassen, 1991, cited in Goe, 1994). In order to overcome this problem, respondent firms/establishments were asked to describe briefly their core service activities. Firms, which cater primarily for final consumers, were subsequently eliminated.

1.6. Research Design

With particular reference to the objectives listed above, the study reported here adopted the following research strategies and methodology, namely:

(a) Conducted a literature review and prepared a synthesis of the principal findings of previous research on aspects such as the role of services in the urban economy, its sectoral and locational characteristics in the context of economic and social restructuring,

(b) Carried out aggregate data analysis using secondary data to unravel the contribution of producer services to urban economic growth,

(c) Still using secondary data, a more detailed sectoral analysis was conducted to illustrate some of the key issues of producer services development in an urban context,

(d) Detailed face-to-face interviews with top management of establishment within the producer services category, representatives of professional organizations, and government officials engaged in regulatory and promotional activities.

1.7. Survey Methodology

The survey consisted of several phases, spread over a period of 14 months from September 1997 to October 1998. The first survey instrument was mailed in September 1997 consisting a total of 203 sampled establishments, which represent 25 percent of the estimated total producer services establishments in Kuala Lumpur. This phase was designed to obtain detailed primary data on service establishments. The survey instrument consisted of a structured questionnaire that sought information concerning service establishment/organization profile, locational characteristics, operational aspect, service strategy, firm's perception of factors leading to increasing demands for producer services in the marketplace, and their assessment of regulatory environment and government policies for the promotion of export of services. A second postal survey was conducted in October 1997, covering another 324 sampled establishments.

As this method of survey achieved neither a good response rate nor a satisfactory quality of responses, face-to-face interviews were also carried out in order to elicit detailed aspects of respondents firms operation. Followed up phone interviews had to be made in order to fill up gaps in information provided.

Detailed interviews with firms representing each sub-sector, with regulatory authorities and professional organizations were carried out between April and October 1998. These represent in-depth investigations into specific issues. Although a common questionnaire was not used, a series of issues were addressed in each interview. However, these had to be treated with some flexibility. Information from each interview was presented in this report in the form of several case studies.

1.8. Sample Structure

Producer services establishments were sampled from Business Times/Malaysian Industrial Development Authority (MIDA) *1994 Directory of Services*, and *The Malaysian Services for Export, 1997* produced by the Malaysia External Trade Development Corporation (MATRADE). A stratified random sample was then undertaken. As noted earlier, for the first mailing a total of 203 producer service establishments were contacted by letter; subsequently students assistants were employed as field workers to check completed questionnaires at locations and subsequently collect them. This resulted in only 29 valid survey completions. A second postal survey was conducted on 324 producer services establishments. Some of these establishments were already sampled in the first phase, but because of incomplete addresses and delivery problems, the establishments failed to respond to our survey. Fieldwork has enabled us to locate these establishments for the second postal survey. In addition to this, replacement establishments were identified and questionnaires were delivered. There were 25 establishments that fall in this category (Table 1.0). Three hundred twenty four establishments were contacted by letters, resulting in 38 being duly completed and returned. However, some returned questionnaires needed follow-up through phone interviews.

As at the end of the survey period there were 92 valid survey completions. Some returned questionnaires have to be excluded because it is evidently clear from their responses that they were not producer services firms according to our research definition. Their main clients are final consumers.

1.9. Secondary Data

Secondary data for the first stage of the research were requested from the Department of Statistics, Malaysia. These were in both published and unpublished data from 1984 and 1994 Census of Professional and Institutional Establishment - Private Sector, and the 1984 and 1992 Census of Selected Service Industries.

Table 1.0 Producer Services Establishments in Kuala Lumpur: Sample Structure

Sub-Sectors	Total	First Mailing			Second Mailing			(By Hand)
		Total Mailed	Total Responded	%	Total Mailed	Total Responded	%	Respondents Not on List
Advertising/Public Relations	80	22	2	9.1	27	2	7.4	2
Accountancy	88	24	4	16.7	40	3	7.5	3
Architect	3	2	0	0.0	0	0	none	1
Banking	72	16	1	6.3	29	7	24.1	1
Engineering	42	12	2	16.7	22	5	22.7	1
Finance	50	12	1	8.3	18	3	16.7	0
INSURANCE	149	20	3	15.0	65	4	6.2	2
Legal	103	16	3	18.8	41	3	7.3	6
IT	3	3	0	0.0	0	0	none	4
Telecommunication	5	5	1	20.0	0	0	none	0
Management Consultancy	21	21	5	23.8	1	0	0.0	4
Printing	4	4	1	25.0	0	0	none	0
Marketing Research	5	5	0	0.0	0	0	none	0
Real Estate	143	20	2	10.0	79	11	13.9	1
Taxation	25	21	4	19.0	0	0	none	0
Building Construction/Surveyor	4	0	0	none	2	0	0.0	0
Total	**797**	**203**	**29**	**14.3**	**324**	**38**	**11.7**	**25**

Total Respondents = 92

1.10. Scope and Coverage of Study

As noted earlier, in the research reported here, the term "producer services" is operationally defined to include only two major groups of activities i.e. finance, insurance, real estate, and business/professional services (FIREB). Table 1.0 identifies the specific sub-sectors in these two groups. Due to the relatively small number of respondent firms in some sub-sectors, for analytical purposes the two major groups will not be desegregated. For the purpose of further clarification, the two major groups are referred to as "producer services" due to the fact that they supply intermediate inputs to other economic sectors and also to the service sector itself. Unlike consumer services these activities play a very important role in stimulating urban economic growth.

Chapter 2

SERVICES IN THE MALAYSIAN ECONOMY

2.1. INTRODUCTION

The primary aim of this chapter is to assemble some empirical evidence on the growing economic importance of the services sector (and producer services, in particular) in Malaysia. It has to be noted at the outset that any attempt to present a satisfactory statistical coverage of the growth trend and pattern of the services sector is very difficult. This is especially so in the case of producer services. Data for this sector are relatively scarce compared to the manufacturing sector (see for example, Sieh, 1992). Time series analysis is impossible as a result of statistical revision and re-definition of pertinent variables, and perhaps more importantly, non-availability of time-series data itself. The importance of services in the Malaysian economy could only be best illustrated by means of employment data, its contribution to the GDP and commercial banks lending or investment in this sector.

2.2. SERVICES AND BALANCE OF PAYMENT (BOP) PROBLEMS

Recent problems relating to deficit in the services account of the balance of payments has brought to the fore the need to examine very closely policy options and future measures with respect to the services sector in general. According to the Bank Negara Malaysia (the Central Bank) Annual Report for 1995, the overall balance of payments registered a deficit of RM4.4 billion following a deficit of RM8.3 billion in 1994. The current account deteriorated further in 1995 to record a deficit of RM17.8 billion or 8.8 percent of GNP (1994: RM11 billion or 6.2 percent of GNP), due to a significantly reduced surplus in the merchandise account and the widening of the services deficit (see Table 2.0).

The major factor contributing to the deficit in BOP included higher payments for freight and insurance associated with continuing strong growth in imports and higher payments on investment income, reflecting higher accruals of profit and dividends to foreign investors operating in Malaysia. Nevertheless, the higher outflows on these components were moderated to some extent by high receipts from tourism, contract and professional services, and freight and passenger fares. While the services account has been in deficit, the services sector, including the full range of consumer and producer services, has developed at approximately the same pace as the overall expansion of the economy, with its share of the GDP at 40-45 percent since 1992. Arguably, several factors in the global and city-level environments have contributed to the high demand for services generally and for the producer services in particular. A significant proportion of these demands have emerged as the globalization process has had an impact on Malaysia, and effect reinforced by the expressed desires of local leadership to re-position Kuala Lumpur in the global web of cities (see Morshidi and Suriati, 1999). Rising demands for new business services are also due to new developments in communication technologies and computerization. The latter has emerged from the greater externalization of specialized services, a response reflecting the western experience. Transnational firms, some with local partnerships, have been prominent in this development. Recent economic liberalization, privatization, and other deregulation measures and amendments have enabled transnational service firms to participate actively in new and emerging activities and successfully create market niches for themselves in the country (Morshidi, 1998).

Table 2.0. Balance of Payments 1990-2000

Item	RM Million			% of GNP		
	1990	*1995*	*2000*	*1990*	*1995*	*2000*
Merchandise Account	7,093	630	25,876	6.4	0.3	7.5
Exports	77,458	180,956	354,948	69.9	89.4	103.2
Imports	70,365	180,326	329,072	63.5	89.1	95.7
Services Account	-9,723	-18,845	-24,479	-8.8	-9.3	-7.1
Freight & Insurance	-3,837	-8,835	-7,521	-3.5	-4.4	-2.2
Other Transportation	-25	672	2,518	-0.0	0.3	0.6
Travel	632	4,900	3,964	0.6	2.4	1.2
Investment Income	-5,072	-11,208	-16,732	-4.6	-5.5	-4.9
Government Transaction	-3	-45	-60	-0.0	-0.0	-0.0
Other Services	-1,418	-4,329	-6,288	-1.3	-2.1	-1.8
Transfers	147	400	439	0.1	0.2	0.1
Current Account	-2,483	-17,815	1,836	-2.2	-8.8	0.5

Source: The STAR, 8 December 1997

Another important reason for the growth of producer services has been the Government's policy designed to develop services that are actually at the forefront of innovation, especially those concerning new IT. This is based on a belief that new IT-based services, such as software and telematics, are triggers to innovation across the economy, creating substantially different effects to earlier innovations from manufacturing industry (see Miles, 1993). Furthermore, as Coffey and Bailly (1992) have argued, the externalization of some service functions by firms has intertwined manufacturing industry (see Miles, 1993). Furthermore, as Coffey and Bailly (1992) have argued, the externalization of some service functions by firms has intertwined manufacturing and services more intensively, generating more growth in producer services. The Malaysian government is creating a conducive situation for this to happen in the IT sector.

2.3. Growth of Services in the Malaysian Economy - An Overview of Trend and Pattern

In the 1980s, services sector emerged as the second most important source of economic growth after the manufacturing sector (Table 2.1). Since 1990, the promotion of private sector activity as the main engine of growth, and the liberalization and deregulation of the economy have undoubtedly contributed to a structural transformation process as displayed in the data in Table 2.1 and Table 2.2.

The share of the services sector has been maintained at about 40-45 percent of the GDP for about three decades and in 1995 its contribution amounted to about 44 percent (the 1997 figure was actually 44.9 percent of the GDP). The services sector comprises diverse sub-sectors ranging from the transport, storage and communications and finance, insurance, real estate and business services sub-sectors, which provide intermediate services to the wholesale and retail trade, hotels and restaurants, utilities, and government services sub-sectors that produce final services.

A closer examination of the various sub-sectors will reveal some important developments. In the 1960s and 1970s, the development of the services sector was focused on basic infrastructure facilities such as utilities, transportation and government services. Since the late 1980s, between 1989 and 1996 however, producer services gained more importance. The most impressive development within the producer services sector is the performance of the finance, insurance, real estate and business sub-sectors (FIREB), which in 1995, became the second most important with a share of the GDP of 10.7 percent. (Notice the annual growth rates of the Finance, Insurance, Real Estate and Business Services Sub-Sector in Figure 2.1). In addition, its share of employment has jumped from 1 percent to almost 5 percent in the last 25 years. Producer services taken together have increased from 9.7 percent of GDP in 1960 to 18 percent by 1995. Final or consumer services on the other hand have declined from 34.9 percent to 26.3 percent over the same period. Evidently, service industry expansion has been very selective and has mainly taken place in these sub-sectors, which would normally be categorized as "producer services". Growth in producer services evidently indicates a growing demand for such services form other firms, implying that this is an increasing dependence of economic activity on these services.

Table 2.1. Malaysia: Contribution of Services Sector, 1960-1995

Sector	1960		1970		1995	
	% of GDP	% of Employment	% of GDP	% of Employment	% of GDP	% of Employment
Intermediate Services	9.7	4.3	13.7	4.3	18.0	9.6
Finance, Insurance, real estate and business services[1]	6.1	n.a.	8.8	0.9	10.7	4.6
Transport, storage and communication	3.6	n.a.	4.9	3.4	7.3	5.0
Final Services	34.9	33.4	29.9	27.2	26.2	37.4
Utilities	1.3	n.a.	1.9	0.8	2.4	0.6
Wholesale and retail trade, hotels and restaurants	15.7	n.a.	13.8	10.9	12.1	17.5
Government services	6.5	n.a.	11.6	11.7	9.7	11.1
Other services	11.4	n.a.	2.6	3.8	2.0	8.2
Total services	44.6	37.7	43.6	31.5	44.2	47.0

[1]Includes owner occupied dwellings

Source: Bank Negara Malaysia, 1995. *Annual Report*, in Sulaiman Mahbob and P. Rawindram Nair, 1996. *Deficit in the Services Account of the Balance of Payment*, Malaysian Institute of Economic Research; Kuala Lumpur. : 2.

Table 2.2. Gross Domestic Product by Industry of Origin, 1985-2000

Sector	RM million (in 1978)				Average Annual Growth Rate (%)			Share of GDP (%)			
	1985	1990	1995	2000	5th Malaysia Plan	6th Malaysia Plan	Target 7th Malaysia Plan	1985	1990	1995	2000
Agriculture, Forestry, Livestock & Fishing	11,854	14,827	16,406	18,460	4.6	2.0	2.4	20.8	18.7	13.6	10.5
Mining & Quarrying	5,958	7,757	8,938	10,023	5.2	2.9	2.3	10.4	9.8	7.4	5.7
Manufacturing	11,063	21,340	39,825	66,251	13.7	13.3	10.7	19.7	26.9	33.1	37.5
Construction	2,738	2,832	5,277	8,560	0.4	13.3	10.2	4.8	3.6	4.4	4.8
Electricity, Gas & Water	948	1,526	2,823	4,686	9.8	13.3	10.7	1.7	1.9	2.3	2.7
Transport, Storage & Communications	3,630	5,487	8,787	14,599	8.6	9.9	10.7	6.4	6.9	7.3	8.3
Wholesale & Retail Trade, Hotels & Restaurants	6,911	8,806	14,568	22,378	4.7	10.6	9.0	12.1	11.1	12.1	12.7
Finance, Insurance, Real Estate & Business Services	5,121	7,758	12,884	20,977	8.4	10.7	10.2	9.0	9.8	10.1	11.9
Government Services	6,957	8,447	11,683	14,354	4.0	6.7	4.2	12.2	10.6	9.7	8.1
Other Services	1,301	1,678	2,436	3,749	4.9	7.7	9.0	2.3	2.1	2.0	2.1
(-) Imputed Bank Service	1,834	4,076	8,414	13,242	17.0	15.6	9.5	3.2	5.1	7.0	7.5
Charges	2,246	2,947	5,101	5,840	5.8	11.6	2.7	3.9	3.7	4.3	3.2
(+) Import Duties											
GDP at Purchasers' Value	57,093	79,329	120,316	176,635	6.7	8.7	8.0	100.0	100.0	100.0	100.0
Adjusted for Import Duties less Imputed Bank Service											
Charges	17,942	22,267	24,665	27,337	1.5	.1	2.1	31.4	28.1	20.5	15.5
PRIMARY SECTOR	14,102	23,832	43,894	71,802	11.9	11.9	10.3	24.7	30.0	36.5	40.6
SECONDARY SECTOR	25,049	33,230	51,757	77,496	9.1	9.1	8.4	43.9	41.9	43.0	43.9
TERTIARY SECTOR											

Source: Government of Malaysia, 1991: 22; Government of Malaysia, 1996: 52

It is important to note that despite the above-mentioned positive developments in the services sector, Malaysia is still a net importer of services other than tourism, and this has contributed to the deficit in the country's current account of the balance of payments, discussed earlier. (By the end of 1996 this situation has not improved, and arguably the present currency crisis could be attributable to the current account problems, see also Table 2.0).

Employment growth in the services sector has also recorded a dramatic shift. In particular, the share to total employment of intermediate services, which has remained constant between 1960 and 1970, has more than doubled by 1995 (Table 2.3). While the share of employment in agriculture has declined in significance since the 1970s, both the services and the manufacturing sectors have gained importance. By 1980, the services sector became the largest employer in the country. In 1995 close to one-half of the labour force was engaged in the services sector, while the manufacturing sector accounted for about 26 percent of employment. Table 2.3 also summarizes the immediate past and expected future pattern of employment shifts between sectors. More detailed analysis in the National Plan shows these shifts will be accompanied by changes in the pattern of employment by occupational types. The National Plan anticipates Malaysia expects a rise in professional and technical jobs, but it also anticipates production workers will continue to be a major category of workers (Morshidi, 1998).

The importance of the services sector for the Malaysian economy is further revealed by the direction of credit to the services sector since 1990 (Table 2.4). Transport and Storage, Finance, Insurance and Business Services, and other services accounted for 11.6 percent of total lending of RM2.6 billion in 1995. In 1990, the same services sector accounted for 14.1 percent of total lending of RM1.2 billion. In fact, from Table 2.3 the three services sub-sectors noted above have been expanding rapidly between 1991 and 1995.

Figure 2.1. Services Sector: Annual Growth Rate by Sub-Sectors, 1989-1997

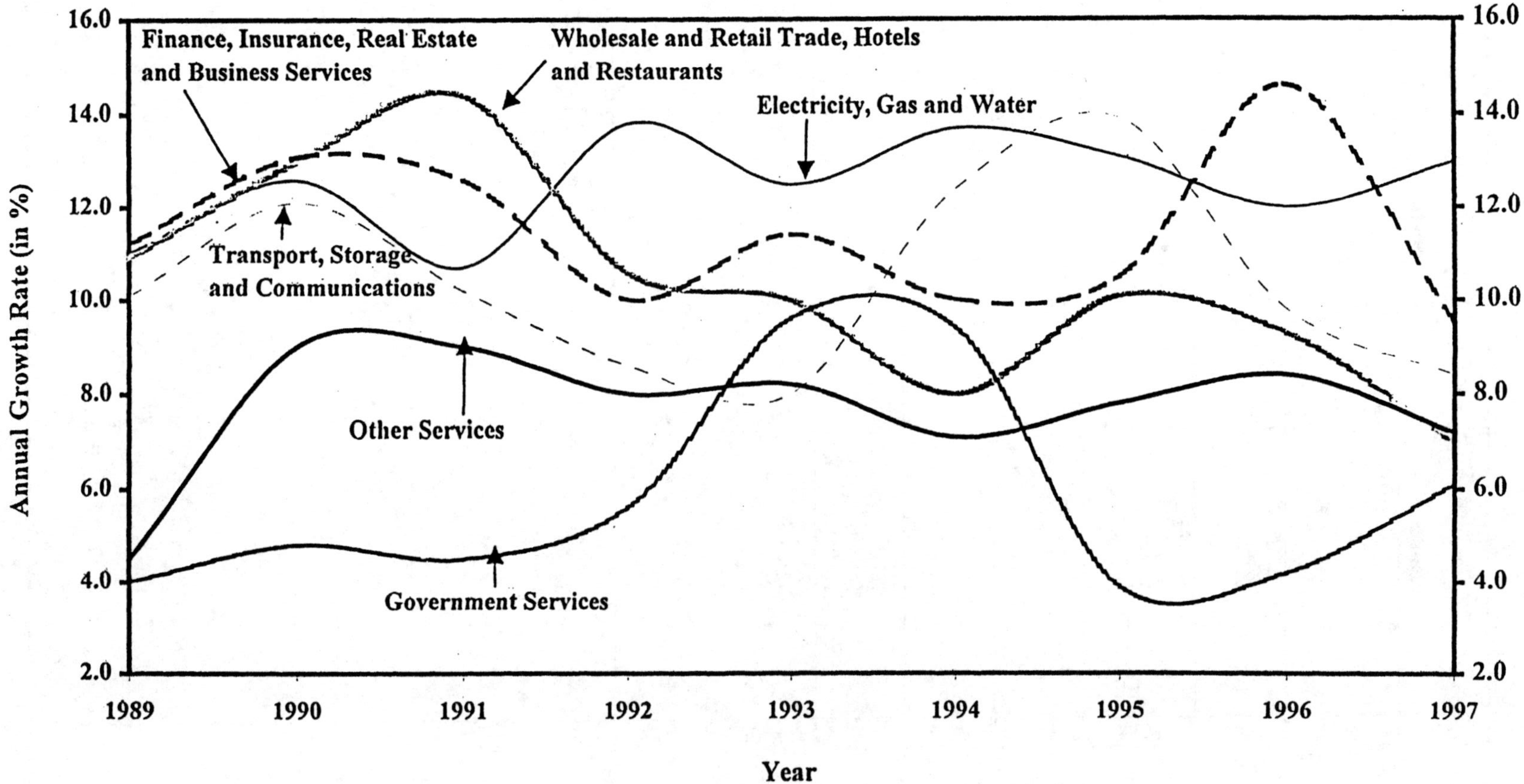

Source: Ministry of Finance, Malaysia. Economic Report – various issues

Table 2.3. Malaysia: Employment by Sector, 1990-2000 ('000 persons)

Sector							*Average Annual Growth Rate (%)*		*Net Job Creation*			
	1990	*%*	*1995*	*%*	*2000*	*%*	*6MP*	*7MP*	*6MP*	*%*	*7MP*	*%*
Agriculture, Forestry, Livestock & Fishing	1,738.0	26.0	1,428.7	18.0	1,187.7	13.1	-3.8	-3.6	-309.3	-25.2	-241.0	-20.9
Mining & Quarrying	37.0	0.6	40.7	0.5	44.5	0.5	1.9	1.8	3.7	0.3	3.8	0.3
Manufacturing	1,333.0	19.9	2,051.6	25.9	2,616.3	28.9	9.0	5.0	718.6	58.5	564.7	49.1
Construction	424.0	6.3	659.4	8.3	845.4	9.3	9.2	5.1	235.4	19.1	186.0	16.2
Electricity, Gas & Water	47.0	0.7	69.1	0.9	84.0	0.9	8.0	4.0	22.1	1.8	14.9	1.3
Transport, Storage & Communications	302.0	4.5	395.2	5.0	506.9	5.6	5.5	5.1	93.2	7.6	111.7	9.7
Wholesale & Retail Trade, Hotel & Restaurants	1,218.0	18.2	1,327.8	16.8	1,469.6	16.2	1.7	2.1	109.8	8.9	141.8	12.3
Finance, Insurance, Real Estate & Business Services	258.0	3.9	378.5	4.8	479.0	5.3	8.0	4.8	120.5	9.8	100.5	8.7
Government Services	850.0	12.7	872.2	11.0	894.2	9.9	0.5	0.5	22.2	1.8	22.0	1.9
Other Services	479.0	7.2	692.2	8.7	938.6	10.4	7.6	6.3	213.2	17.3	246.4	21.4
Total	6,686.0	100.0	7,915.4	100.0	9,066.2	100.0	3.4	2.8	1,229.4	100.0	1,150.8	100.0
Labour Force	*7,042.0*		*8,140.0*		*9,327.1*		*2.9*	*2.8*				
Local	*6,752.0*		*7,490.0*		*8,546.1*		*2.1*	*2.7*				
Foreign	*290.0*		*650.0*		*781.0*		*17.5*	*3.7*				
Unemployment	*356.0*		*224.6*		*260.9*							
Unemployment Rate (%)	*5.1*		*2.8*		*2.8*							

Source: Government of Malaysia, 1996. *The Seventh Malaysia Plan, 1996-2000.* : 110

Table 2.4. Loans to Major Sectors by the Banking System (RM Million)

Sector	*1990*	*(%)*	*1995*	*(%)*	*Average Annual Growth Rate, 1991-95*
Agriculture	5,649	4.9	5,245	2.0	-1.5
Mining & Quarrying	1,069	0.9	1,184	0.5	2.1
Manufacturing	21,540	18.6	48,752	18.7	17.7
Electricity	238	0.2	3,750	1.4	73.5
General Commerce	13,552	11.7	21,400	8.2	9.6
Real Estate & Construction	21,066	18.2	40,201	15.4	13.8
Housing	14,897	12.8	33,092	12.7	17.3
Transport & Storage	2,440	2.1	5,096	2.0	15.9
Finance, Insurance & Business Services	12,057	10.4	31,815	12.2	21.4
Other Services	1,826	1.6	6,853	2.6	30.3
Purchase of Stocks & Shares	3,021	2.6	13,350	5.1	34.6
Consumption Credit	11,695	10.1	30,198	11.6	20.9
Others	6,903	6.0	19,916	7.6	23.6
Total	**115,953**	**100.0**	**260,852**	**100.0**	**17.6**

Source: Government of Malaysia, 1996: 479

2.4. SERVICE ACTIVITIES - SOME SALIENT FEATURES

The following analysis is based on data from the Census of Selected Service Industries, 1984 and 1992. Table 2.5 summarizes the main trend of the various services activities. Based on the number of companies established between the years 1984 and 1992, five of eleven services sectors displayed some expanding trends, with the road haulage sector identified as having the most intense growth during the eight-year period.

Table 2.5. Performance of Selected Services Industries in Malaysia, 1984-1992

Services Industries	*Expanding/Declining*	*% Change*
Shipping Companies	Declining	-26.9
Real Estate Agents	Expanding	+23.77
Bus Transport	Declining	-2.5
Road Haulage	Expanding	+63
Cinemas	Declining	-8.3
Tourist and Travel Agencies	Expanding	+19.7
Shipping Agents	Expanding	+39.3
Stock Brokers, Commodity Brokers and Foreign Exchange Brokers	Declining	-1
Stevedoring Companies	Declining	-12.8
Advertising Agencies	Declining	-11.6
Hotels and Other Lodging Places	Expanding	+36

Source: Department of Statistics Malaysia, 1986; 1997

The five growing sectors are (a) road haulage with 5626 to 9158 companies in 1984 and 1992 respectively, a growth of 63 percent, (b) shipping agents from 282 to 393 companies in 1984 and 1992 respectively, a growth of 39.3 percent, (c) hotels and other lodging places from 1021 to 1386 companies in 1984 and 1992 respectively, a growth of 36 percent, (d) real estate agents from 198 to 245 companies in 1984 and 1992 respectively, a growth of 23.1 percent and (e) tourist and travel agencies from 757 to 906 companies in 1984 and 1992 respectively, a growth of 19.7 percent.

While the six declining sectors based on number of companies between the year 1984 to 1992 are (a) shipping companies from 350 to 256 companies in 1984 and 1992 respectively, a decline of 26.9 percent, (b) stevedoring companies from 148 to 129 companies in 1984 and 1992 respectively, a decline of 11.6 percent, (d) cinemas from 251 to 230 companies in 1984 and 1992, a decline of 8.3 percent, (e) bus transport from 446 to 435 companies in 1984 and 1992, a decline of 2.5 percent, and (f) stock, commodity and foreign exchange brokers from 95 to 94 companies in 1984 and 1992, a decline of 1 percent.

With respect to labour involvement, generally there is an average of 80 percent increase in labour involvement in the five growing sectors. However, it should be noted that other declining sectors also demonstrated increase in total labour involvement excluding cinemas and stevedoring companies.

The tourist and travel agencies experienced a one fold labour growth of 112.6 percent in this eight-year period, from 4,823 persons employed in 1984 to 10,255 persons employed in 1992. The hotels and other lodging places sub-sector had a 95 percent growth of total labour, from 28,602 persons employed in 1984 to 55,828 persons employed in 1992. Real estates agents also showed a labour increase of 84.2 percent in this eight-year period, with total labour of 810 persons in 1984 to 1,492 persons in 1992. The shipping agents sub-category had a 62.9 percent more labour in 1992 totalling 4,788 persons than in 1984 of 2,940 people. Meanwhile, the road haulage had a 75 percent increase in total labour involved in the sector, from 28,773 persons employed in 1984 to 50,342 persons employed in 1992.

The most growth in labour head count is identified in the stock, commodity and foreign exchange brokers sub-sector and this is despite the declining rate of 1 percent in number of companies established nationwide. In 1984, the sector reported a total of 3,229 person employed while in 1992 it reached 11,537, a twofold growth of 257 percent.

Other declining sectors that experienced growth in total labour involvement are the advertising agencies, bus transport and shipping companies. The advertising agencies, recorded a 49.7 percent growth, from 2,475 persons employed in 1984 to 3,705 in 1992. The bus transport and shipping companies reported a 1.6 percent and 11.4 percent respectively in labour growth. The former, which had 25,644 persons employed in 1984 increased its total labour force to 26,048 persons in 1992, and, the latter which had 10,759 persons employed in 1984 also increased its total labour force to 11,986 persons in 1992.

The two declining sectors that showed reduction in total labour involvement are the cinemas, with the highest declining rate, and the stevedoring companies. In a period of ten years, the cinemas recorded a declining rate of 38 percent in total labour force, from 3,042 persons employed in 1984 to only 1,873 total persons employed in 1992. While the stevedoring companies reported a total of 8,712 persons employed in 1992 from a total of 8,824 persons employed in 1984.

2.5. Producer (Professional) Services in Malaysia, 1984-1994 - Some Salient Features

Data from the Census of Professional and Institutional Establishments-Private Sector - of 1984 and 1994 indicates that five out of six professional services activities experienced growth, in terms of number of establishments and employment between 1984 and 1994. The building draughtsmen service activity was the only one experiencing contraction in both of these aspects.

2.5.1 Expanding Professional Services Activities in Malaysia

The five professional services activities in descending growth order are lawyers, architects, engineers, surveyors and accountants. Besides growth in number of establishments, these five professional services also showed positive change in total employment in the period between 1984 and 1994.

For the same period, the legal services establishment in Malaysia grew by a significant 86.25 percent, from 989 services establishments to 1842 services establishments. Total persons employed also increased by a high 118.23 percent from 10,138 persons employed as on 31st December 1984 to 22,124 persons employed as on 31st December 1994. The more than one fold increased in labour force for the legal services establishments represented the highest growth in total employment among the professional services activities.

Also noted for its high growth performance are the architectural services (72.64 percent growth in number of establishments). In 1984, there were 318 architectural establishments, and, in 1994 the number grew to 549 establishments. Total persons employed in 1984 and 1994 were 4,355 persons and 7,009 persons respectively, a growth of 60.94 percent, placing it as the third highest in the employment growth rate after the engineering services establishments.

Meanwhile, the engineering services establishments recorded the third highest growth rate in terms of number of establishments - a 48.92 percent growth with a total of 325 engineering firms in 1984 and 484 engineering firms ten years later. However, in terms of labour expansion, it fell second to the legal services establishments. The engineering establishments' labour force grew more than one half in the ten-year period at 69.91 percent, with 7,929 persons employed as of end of 1984 and 13,472 persons employed as at the end of December 1994.

Other growing professional services establishments - surveyors and accountants - have experienced a growth rate of 32.74 percent and 28.59 percent, respectively. In 1984 and 1994, there were 339 and 450 surveyors' services establishments in Malaysia, correspondingly. Total employment for the surveyor services establishments grew at 43.99 percent in ten years, from 7,165 total persons employed to 10,317 total persons employed. As for accountancy services, there were 731 firms in 1984 and ten years later, there were 940 firms in Malaysia. Total employment for this activity recorded a 56.94 percent growth in ten years, from 9,268 persons employed to 14,545 persons employed.

2.5.2. Declining Professional Services Activities in Malaysia

The building draughtsmen services activity was experiencing a downturn during the ten-year period - in terms of total number of establishments and total persons employed. Although the aggregate data showed that this activity experienced only a 6 percent reduction in number of establishments, its labour force dropped by a substantial 23.33 percent. In 1984, there were a total of 198 establishments offering this service employing

643 persons, but in 1994, as mentioned above, the number of establishments has dropped to 187 with only 493 persons employed.

2.6. NET INCOME CONTRIBUTION OF PROFESSIONAL SERVICES ACTIVITIES IN MALAYSIA, 1984-1994

Nationwide, the share of net income contribution has decreased in four of the six professional service activities during the ten-year period from 1984 to 1994. The service establishments experiencing contraction in the net income contributions were the accounting, architect, building draughtsmen and legal services. The rest, engineering and surveyors service establishments have shown commendable increase in contribution towards the total net income for Malaysia.

2.6.1 Professional Services Establishments Experiencing Increase in Net Income Contribution

In 1984, the engineering service establishment had a total net income of RM29, 772,000 which made up only 16.75 percent of total net income for Malaysia of RM177, 691,000 for the six professional services activities. However, in 1994, engineering service establishments recorded RM945, 737,000 in net income for the year, which represented 31.50 percent of total net income of RM3, 002,128,000 for the six professional services activities in Malaysia. The engineering service establishments, then, also demonstrated a remarkable 88.06 percent improvement in net income contribution during the ten-year period, from 16.75 percent in 1984 to 31.50 percent in 1994.

Another significant professional services establishments that showed the same pattern in percentage of net income contribution relative to other activities was the surveyor service establishment, which reported RM15, 482,000 in net income in 1984, representing 8.71 percent of the total net income for Malaysia's six selected professional services activities, and, RM436, 091,000 in net income in 1994, representing 14.53 percent of the total net income for Malaysia's six professional services activities. These showed a marked improvement of 66.82 in percentage of net income contributed by the surveyor services establishments in ten years.

2.6.2 Professional Services Establishments Experiencing Decrease in Net Income Contribution

The other four professional service establishments, accountants, architects, legal and building draughtsmen, experienced decline in share of net income at around 20 percent to 30 percent with the exception of building draughtsmen which experienced a drastic 71.57 percent reduction in percentage of net income contributed during the ten-year period from 1984 to 1994. The building draughtsmen service establishments contributed only 1.02 percent equivalent of RM1, 813,000 of the total net income for Malaysia of RM177,

691,000 in 1984. However, ten years later, it contributed only a modest 0.29 percent (RM8, 833,000) of the total net income for Malaysia's six professional services establishments.

The accountancy service establishments' net income share of 18.49 percent (RM32, 849,000) dropped to 14.43 percent (RM433, 144,000) of the total net income for Malaysia in 1984 and 1994, respectively. Thus, a negative change of 21.96 percent in ten years. Similarly, architectural service establishments reported a drop in percentage of net income contribution by 27.84 percent in ten years from 18.57 percent (RM32, 998,000) of total net income for Malaysia in 1984 to 13.40 percent (RM402, 431,000) of total net income for Malaysia in 1994. Lastly, the legal service establishments, despite intense growth in employment and number of establishments, also showed a drop in share of net income from 36.45 percent (RM64, 777,000) to 25.84 percent (RM775, 892,000) of the total net income for the nation's six professional services establishments in 1984 and 1994, a 29.11 percent decline in share of net income contributed for the ten-year period.

2.7. Government Policies and Strategies Towards the Services Sector

The Seventh Malaysia Plan, 1996-2000 pursued and implemented policies and strategies aimed at transforming the services sector into a major catalyst of growth as well as a potential export sector. In the finance sector, measures were taken to enable it to be more innovative and dynamic to meet the needs of the real estate sector, which provided the space buildings for service sector location. The major thrust for the insurance industry were aimed at upgrading its financial strength, efficiency, skills and productivity. Policy measures were focused on key areas such as capital requirements, cost-effective management, excellent delivery of services and technical competence. In the tourism sector, efforts were intensified to increase visitors' volume, and diversification into new products and services to cater for the varying demands and interest of international and domestic tourists.

Arguably, growth of producer services (in terms of contribution to GNP) in Malaysia still trails that of the growth of the manufacturing sector. However, the potential for the producer services sector to grow in tandem with the manufacturing sector is clearly identified by the *Manufacturing Plus Plus* strategy of the Second Industrial Master plan whereby industrial development is premised on the cluster approach which will promote specific industries in an integrated and synergised manner and spur the development of higher value added activities. Generally, the *Manufacturing Plus Plus* strategy calls for the participation of domestic service suppliers in the whole value-chain of a product. Some of the intermediate services identified for the *Manufacturing Plus Plus* strategy are as follows:

(a) Conventional business services of finance and accounting, legal, public relations, advertising and marketing.

(b) Technical business services of quality control, testing, environmental management services, management consulting and production consulting.
(c) Information technology, involving data processing, management information systems, electronic data interchange and networks systems.
(d) R & D in software developments, industrial design and product development.
(e) Marketing involving the printing and publishing services.

Hence, the Malaysian government's policy will probably spur the growth of the services sector, particularly the producer services sub-sector. More importantly, if successful these policies will continue the spatial changes already felt in major metropolitan areas where higher concentrations of producer services activities are to be found.

2.8. CONCLUSION

There is no doubt that service activities are slowly becoming very important in the Malaysia economy. Producer services have accounted for a substantial majority of service growth since 1985, and they are very important for the growth of metropolitan economy. It is in the metropolitan areas such as Kuala Lumpur that the highest proportion of producer service jobs to be found – both in terms of absolute and relative terms. The higher order producer services such as FIREB activities concentrated in Kuala Lumpur relative to Malaysia as a whole. Peripheral distribution of producer services in the country is, as expected, fairly simple. This concentrated pattern of growth in producer services (in Kuala Lumpur and immediate periphery, for example) is expected to continue in the future because of government policy in relation to the development of Kuala Lumpur and the Multi-Media Super Corridor (MSC). Producer services activities have been known to concentrate in large metropolitan areas in order to have access to highly qualified labour, good and modern infra and infostructure, complementary producer services, and large local markets.

Chapter 3

SERVICES GROWTH IN KUALA LUMPUR

3.1. INTRODUCTION

Set against the backdrop of sectoral changes in Malaysia, this chapter will examine the services sector in Kuala Lumpur. In general terms, the Kuala Lumpur's economy can be characterized as an economy experiencing rapid transition to tertiary production as opposed to manufacturing production (see Morshidi and Suriati, 1999). Since 1980s, the rapid transition of Kuala Lumpur's economy has served the territory well: for instance GDP per capita has constantly been higher than for Malaysia as a whole; incomes have also been higher than the rest of the country. What has triggered the shifts in the Kuala Lumpur's economy? To what extent is this shift attributed to growth in producer services activities? What are the salient features of the structure and functioning of Kuala Lumpur's producer services? In order to answer some of these questions, statistics specific to Kuala Lumpur in two censuses - (a) Census of Selected Service Industries, 1984 and 1992, and (b) Census of Professional and Institutional Establishments - Private Sector - 1984 and 1994 - will be utilized. However, because of data scarcity, only partial answers to the above questions are to be found upon analysis of the census data.

3.2. KUALA LUMPUR - TOWARDS A SERVICE ECONOMY?

The services sector contributed 83 percent of the total value added of Kuala Lumpur, and grew at a rate of 10.1 percent per annum since 1990 (Government of Malaysia, 1996). The rapid growth of this sector was due to the expansion of four service industry groups (finance, insurance, real estate and business services; estate and business services; wholesale and retail trade, hotels and restaurants as well as transport, storage and communications), which collectively accounted for no less than 60 percent of all new jobs in the city. However, there were in fact substantial variations in the performances of the different types of services, as they have not been expanding at the same rate.

On the one hand, retailing and consumer services have in fact grown steadily reflecting, to a certain extent, the changing taste and consumption patterns of the population of Kuala Lumpur. Growth in producer services, on the other hand, is best seen as a result of increasing demand for such services from other establishments, implying an increasing dependence of the Kuala Lumpur's economy on these services. But producer services such as finance, insurance, real estate and business services have contributed most to the expansion in the service sector value added and employment. Public services, although employing more people, contributed proportionately less to state GDP. Producer services aside, employment in other services grew by leaps and bound because of lower productivity growth in the other services category. Evidently, the services sector take on relatively more workers, thus producing a shift in the distribution of employment.

3.3. Kuala Lumpur - Services Sector Growth

The nationwide trend in services sector growth presented in the preceding chapter also extended to Kuala Lumpur with some sub-sector growth reflecting or surpassing the nation's growth rate. For instance, in terms of number of establishments, the road haulage sector in Kuala Lumpur grew 62.9 percent, from a total of 361 companies in 1984 to a total of 588 companies in 1992, reflecting that of the nation's growth of 63 percent. According to the Census in 1992, 6.4 percent of 9,158 road haulage establishments in Malaysia are to be found in Kuala Lumpur. Another services sector that mirrored the growth nationally is the shipping agents, which had a 36.4 percent growth in the number of companies between 1984 and 1992. There were 11 shipping agents in Kuala Lumpur in 1984 and this has increased to 15 in 1992 representing only 3.8 percent of a total of 393 shipping agents in Malaysia.

Interestingly, the tourist and travel agencies in Kuala Lumpur displayed commendable growth of 38.3 percent in the number of companies established in the eight-year period covered by the Census, which doubled the national growth rate of 19.7 percent for the same industries. This growth has resulted in the number of agencies increasing to 325 from 235 eight years earlier. However, it should be noted that there is a slight decline of about 5 percent in the percentage of tourist and travel agencies in Kuala Lumpur relative to the total number of agencies in Malaysia; 31 percent of a total of 757 agencies in Malaysia in 1984 were in Kuala Lumpur, and this has declined to 26 percent in 1992. In that particular year there were 906 agencies in the country.

Service industries such as real estate agents, hotels and other lodging places demonstrated slower growth rates in Kuala Lumpur than the nation. Kuala Lumpur had 74 agents in 1984 and 84 agents in 1992, and this represents a 13.5 percent increase in the number of agents compared to the national figure of 23.7 percent. In 1984, the 74 agents in Kuala Lumpur represented 37.4 percent of the total 198 agents in Malaysia and eight years later Kuala Lumpur's share increased to 34.3 percent of the total 245 real estate agents in Malaysia.

As for the category hotels and other lodging places in Kuala Lumpur, there is an 11.4 percent increase in number of establishments, in contrast to the nation's higher growth rate of 36 percent. In 1984, there were 132 hotels and other lodging places in Kuala Lumpur (or 13 percent of a total of 1021 in Malaysia) and this has increased to 147 in 1992 (or 10 percent of the total 1386 hotels and other lodgings in the country).

The cinemas sector, and the stock, commodity and foreign exchange brokers sector in Kuala Lumpur recorded a 4.5 percent and 11.6 percent growth respectively despite the negative growth rate of the two sectors nationwide. There were 22 cinemas in Kuala Lumpur in 1984 and 23 cinemas in 1992, which made up 10 percent and 8.8 percent of total number of cinemas in Malaysia in 1984 and 1992 respectively.

Meanwhile, there were 43 establishments operating as stock, commodity and foreign exchange brokers in 1984 and 48 establishments in 1992. From a total of 95 stock, commodity and foreign exchange brokerage establishments in Malaysia in 1984, Kuala Lumpur's share is 45 percent and this has increased to 51 percent in 1992 (total number of establishments were 94 in 1992).

3.4. Kuala Lumpur - Net Income Contribution

Net income contribution from Kuala Lumpur's services sector can be categorized into 3 groups:

(i). Net income that moved positively with growing services.
(ii). Net income that moved negatively with growing services.
(iii). Net income that moved negatively with declining services.

In 1984, the shipping agents in Kuala Lumpur contributed 2.9 percent towards the total net income for the sector. Eight years later, it recorded a 7.5 percent increase in net income contribution, which was 10.4 percent of the total net income for the shipping agents sector. The net income was based on the aggregate sum of 11 and 15 Kuala Lumpur's shipping agents net income for the year 1984 and 1992 respectively. The number of shipping agents in Kuala Lumpur represented 6 percent of the total shipping agents in Malaysia during the eight-year period.

The real estate agents reported a low 0.29 percent net income contribution in 1984, from the 74 Kuala Lumpur-based real estate agents (37.4 percent of total real estate agents in Malaysia). The sector's net income contribution improved to 33.3 percent in 1992, and this came from the 84 real estate agents (34.4 percent of the total real estate agents in Malaysia).

Meanwhile, 1984 was a bad year for the tourist and travel agencies. The nationwide downturn in the sector in 1984 was also evident in Kuala Lumpur - it contributed 88 percent towards the total net income losses for the sector. At that time, there were 235 agencies, 31 percent of the total tourist and travel agencies in Malaysia. Eight years later, as the sector gained momentum, Kuala Lumpur contributed more than 57 percent towards the total net income for the tourist and travel agencies sector in Malaysia. By then, Kuala Lumpur has 325 agencies, which represented 26 percent of the total tourist and travel agencies in Malaysia.

Between 1984 and 1992, industries in Kuala Lumpur, which were growing, were the stocks, commodity and foreign exchange brokers and the cinema sector. The stock, commodity and foreign exchange sector maintained its net income contribution of around 50 percent during the eight-year period. In 1984, the net income contribution from the 43 brokerage establishments in Kuala Lumpur (45 percent of the total brokerage establishments in Malaysia) was 51.2 percent and, in 1992, the net income contribution from the 48 brokerage establishments in Kuala Lumpur (51 percent of the total brokerage establishments in Malaysia) was 55 percent. Since Kuala Lumpur accommodated almost 50 percent of the brokerage establishments in Malaysia, we can say that Kuala Lumpur with its high net income contribution and large concentration of brokerage establishments implied that it played an active role in the stock, commodity and foreign exchange sector. In addition, it also reported a threefold increase in labour involvement of 316 percent in the sector.

Meanwhile, the cinema sector in Kuala Lumpur, despite growth in the number of establishments from 22 in 1984 to 23 in 1992, reported a lower earning in 1992 than in 1984. Its net income contribution fell from 40 percent in 1984 to only 29 percent in 1992. With 22 cinemas in Kuala Lumpur, it has an 8.7 percent share of total cinemas in Malaysia in 1984. In 1992, there were 23 cinemas in Kuala Lumpur, representing 10 percent of the total cinemas in Malaysia. The cinema sector is in the same category as the road haulage sector and the hotels and other lodging places sector which experienced decrease in net income with the increasing number of establishments.

Two industries - the road haulage and the hotels and other lodging places - which are expanding sectors based on number of establishments, contributed less to net income in 1992 than in 1984. The differences in net income contribution between these two years for both sectors are more evident for the hotels and other lodging places industry than the road haulage. Hotels and other lodging places industry noted a 200.6 percent decrease, from 231 percent net income contribution in 1984 to 30.4 percent net income contribution in 1992. Evidently, between the census years, the percentage of companies in Kuala Lumpur relative to other states declined to 10 percent (147 hotels and other lodging places) in 1992 from 13 percent (132 hotels and other lodging places) in 1984.

As for the road haulage sector, the net income contribution dropped from 21.3 percent in 1984 to only 16.4 percent in 1992, even though the number of road haulage companies in Kuala Lumpur increased form 361 to 588 between the census period. Kuala Lumpur also maintained the 6.4 percent road haulage companies concentration relative to other states between these years.

Four other sectors that fall under the third category are bus transport, advertising agencies, stevedoring companies and shipping companies. Bus transport companies in Kuala Lumpur made up 32.5 percent and 26.7 percent of the total bus transport companies in Malaysia in 1984 and 1992 respectively. The 145 bus transport companies contributed RM817, 000 in 1984 despite the losses of RM2, 867,000 reported for the sector. The losses were due to over expenditure by bus transport companies in Kedah, Malacca, Perak, Trengganu and east Malaysia's Sabah and Sarawak. In 1992, the 116 bus transport companies in Kuala Lumpur contributed 30.4 percent of the total net income for the bus transport sector in Malaysia.

For advertising agencies, the net income contribution from Kuala Lumpur dropped, with a 14.3 percent reduction in number of advertising agencies in Kuala Lumpur. In 1984, the net income contribution from the 77 advertising agencies (52.4 percent of Malaysia's total advertising agencies) was 78.3 percent, whereas in 1992, the net income contribution from Kuala Lumpur's 66 advertising agencies (50.8 percent of Malaysia's total advertising agencies) dropped to 66.2 percent of the total net income for the advertising agencies. However, it seems that Kuala Lumpur still played a vital role in the advertising agencies since it contributed more than 50 percent of the total net income for the advertising sector and it also has a marked advertising agencies concentration.

Interestingly, the stevedoring company in Kuala Lumpur also showed strong support in net income contribution for the sector. Data from the 1992 census indicate that there was only one company engaged in stevedoring activities in Kuala Lumpur. (The 1984 Census did not show the exact number of establishments except that there were two stevedoring companies in Selangor). From the total 144 stevedoring companies in Malaysia in 1992, net income contribution from Kuala Lumpur's only stevedoring company amounted to a significant 38.8 percent of the total net income for the stevedoring company sector. In 1992, Kuala Lumpur still had only one stevedoring company (out of the 129 stevedoring companies in Malaysia), but it still reported 12.1 percent of the total net income for Malaysia's stevedoring companies sector.

The shipping companies in Kuala Lumpur, has an important role in terms of net income contribution. Census data indicates that while only 7.7 percent of total shipping companies in Malaysia (or 27 companies) were located in Kuala Lumpur in 1984, this small percentage contributed about 152 percent of the total net income for the shipping companies sector in Malaysia. (The deficit in total net income for the sector was due to over expenditure by all regions except Kedah and Kuala Lumpur). As the sector improved during the eight-year period, all states reported a positive net income with Kuala Lumpur contributing 74.2 percent of the total net income for the shipping companies sector in Malaysia. At that time, Kuala Lumpur had only 11.3 percent of the total shipping companies in Malaysia, represented by 29 shipping companies.

3.5. Professional Services Growth in Kuala Lumpur

Census data indicates that national growth pattern is replicated in Kuala Lumpur, particularly with respect to the number of professional service establishments and employment. In terms of number of establishments operating in Kuala Lumpur, in 1984 Kuala Lumpur had around 13 to 42 percent of the total professional services establishments in Malaysia, while in 1994, the proportion in Kuala Lumpur ranged from 12 to 37 percent of the total professional services establishments in Malaysia. The total employment of each professional services establishment in Kuala Lumpur as a percentage of the total employment in Malaysia for each of the professional services establishment was around 14 to 52 percent in 1984, and 10 to 47 percent in 1994.

3.5.1 Declining Professional Services

Generally, the increase in the number of establishments and employment for each service in Kuala Lumpur mirrored development at the national level, but once again 'building draughtsmen' is the only professional service establishments in Kuala Lumpur that moved against the national trend: a decline in the number of establishments and the number of people employed were recorded between the census period. The building draughtsmen professional service with an 11.54 percent decline in number of establishments also resulted in reduction of 40 percent in its total labour force in a decade. The 26 building draughtsmen establishments operating in Kuala Lumpur had 90 persons employed on 31st December 1984 or 14 percent employed in the same activities nationwide. Ten years later, the 23 building draughtsmen establishments in Kuala Lumpur employed only 54 people as on 31st December 1994, or 10.95 percent of the total 493 persons employed nationwide.

3.5.2 Growing Professional Services

Lawyer's establishments in Kuala Lumpur had the strongest growth in number of establishment of 99.68 percent in a period of ten years. In 1984, Kuala Lumpur recorded 317 legal establishments, but in 1994, Kuala Lumpur had 633 legal establishments. The high growth rate in legal establishments between 1984 and 1994 is also reflected in the total persons employed. The Kuala Lumpur's legal establishments which employed 3,968 persons in 1984, representing 39.14 percent of the total 10,138 persons in this activity, hired 136.01 percent more people in 1994 to a tune of 9,365 persons, equivalent to 42.33 percent of the total 22,124 persons engaged at the national level.

The architectural establishments, which reached 69.60 percent growth in the number of establishments in Kuala Lumpur, ranked fourth in employment growth (51.66 percent) among other Kuala Lumpur's professional service establishments. Kuala Lumpur had 125 architectural service establishments with a total employment of 2,137 persons as on 31st December 1984, equivalent to 49.07 percent of the nation's total 4,355 persons employed in this sector. In 1994, Kuala Lumpur had 212 architectural service establishments with total employment of 3,241 persons as on 31st December, which represented 46.2 percent of the total labour force of 7,009 in Malaysia's architectural establishments.

The surveyor establishments were third in terms of the growth in number of service establishments, but fifth in terms of employment growth. Between 1984 and 1994, the surveyor's establishments grew from 78 establishments to 125 establishments, a growth of 60.26 percent. In terms of total persons employed, by 31st December 1994 the surveyors establishments employed 4,035 persons, which was 48.51 percent more than the total persons employed as of 31st December 1984. The Kuala Lumpur's surveyor's establishments then, employed 37.92 percent of the total 7,165 persons engaged in surveyor's establishments in the country in 1984. In 1994 the sector employed 39.11 percent of the total 10,317 persons engaged in the surveyors establishments nationwide.

Meanwhile, both accounting establishments and engineering establishments have less than 50 percent growth in number of establishments. Between the year 1984 and 1994, the accounting establishments grew at a rate of 34.96 percent and the engineering establishments grew at 25.90 percent. However, growth in total persons employed for both accounting establishments and engineering establishments exceeded 50 percent, at

52.18 percent for the accounting establishments and 53 percent for the engineering establishments during the decade. The accounting establishments recorded 4,481 persons employed as on 31st December under its 226 service establishment in Kuala Lumpur, which represented 48.35 percent of Malaysia's accounting establishments' labour force of 9,268 persons. In 1994, there were 6,819 persons employed with Kuala Lumpur's 305 accountants establishments, which made up 46.88 percent of the Malaysia's accounting establishments' labour force of 14,545 persons. The engineering professional service establishments in Kuala Lumpur, which grew at a rate of 25.90 percent in terms of the number of establishments (from 175 to 139 establishments), employed 4,141 persons as on 31st December 1984, and 6,363 persons as on 31st December 1994. The Kuala Lumpur's engineering establishments' employment relative to the Malaysia's engineering establishments' labour force were 52.23 percent of the total 7,929 persons in 1984, and, 47.23 percent of the total 13,472 person in 1994.

3.6. Net Income Contribution from Kuala Lumpur

Kuala Lumpur's contribution towards the total net income of the six selected professional service establishments in Malaysia selected for this part of the analysis is significant; around 50 percent for both 1984 and 1994, except for the declining building draughtsmen professional service establishments.

The building draughtsmen professional service establishments contributed the least towards the total Kuala Lumpur's professional service establishments' net income, relative to other Kuala Lumpur's professional service establishments. In 1984, the building draughtsmen service establishments' net income of RM224, 000 represented 0.24 percent of Kuala Lumpur's total net income of RM91, 751,000 and in 1994 the Kuala Lumpur building draughtsmen establishments net income contribution was RM1, 182,000 which represented only 0.07 percent of the total Kuala Lumpur's professional service establishments net income for the year. This is a decrease of 0.17 percent in percentage net income contributed from the Kuala Lumpur's building draughtsmen service establishments towards the total Kuala Lumpur's services establishments' net income. It should be noted that there was a 1.02 percent increase in net income contribution from the Kuala Lumpur building draughtsmen establishments towards Malaysia's total net income, despite a decline of 0.83 percent observed in the number of building draughtsmen establishments in Kuala Lumpur. In 1984, Kuala Lumpur owned 13.13 percent (26 building draughtsmen establishments) of the total 198 building draughtsmen establishments in Malaysia, while in 1994; only 12.30 percent (23 building draughtsmen establishments) of the 187 building draughtsmen establishments in Malaysia were located in Kuala Lumpur. In terms of percentage of contribution towards Malaysia's service establishments total net income, the 26 Kuala Lumpur's building draughtsmen establishments' contribution amounted to 12.36 percent in 1984, and, the 23 Kuala Lumpur's building draughtsmen establishments contributed 13.38 percent in 1994.

The highest net income contributor among Kuala Lumpur professional service establishments were the engineering establishments with an impressive 63.54 percent share of the total net income for Malaysia's engineering firm of RM29, 772,000 in 1984. The RM18, 916,000 net income contributions from Kuala Lumpur in 1984 was an aggregate sum from Kuala Lumpur's 139 engineering establishments, which made up 42.77 percent of the nation's total engineering establishments of 325. In 1994, the number of engineering establishments operating in Kuala Lumpur contracted somewhat in terms of number of establishments, and in the net income contribution. In 1994, Kuala Lumpur had a 36.16 percent share of the total 484 engineering establishments in Malaysia - a reduction of 19.81 percent in ten years. The 36.16 percent share or 175 engineering establishments contributed 55.97 percent (RM529, 369,000) towards the total net income of RM945, 737,000 for engineering service establishments in Malaysia. This is still a significant sum, despite a negative 7.57 percent difference after ten years. In contrast, percentage contribution by the Kuala Lumpur's engineering establishments towards the total Kuala Lumpur's net income increased 11.69 percent during the decade. The Kuala Lumpur's engineering establishments contributed 20.62 percent of Kuala Lumpur's total net income of RM91, 751,000 in 1984, and later, in 1994 made the highest contribution, 32.31 percent towards Kuala Lumpur's net income of RM1, 638,202,000.

As mentioned earlier, in 1994, the accountant's professional service establishments in Kuala Lumpur contributed the most towards Malaysia's net income of RM3, 002,128,000. The Kuala Lumpur's accounting establishments, which accounted for 32.45 percent (305 establishments) of the 940 establishments in Malaysia, contributed 56.13 percent (RM243, 144,000) to the total Malaysia's accounting establishments net income of RM433, 144,000. Meanwhile, a decade earlier, Kuala Lumpur which had 30.92 percent (226 establishments) of the total 731 accounting professional service establishments in Malaysia, contributed a net income of 52.99 percent (RM17, 406,000) towards the total Malaysia's accounting establishments net income of RM32, 849,00. Thus, an increase of 3.14 percent in percentage net income contribution from Kuala Lumpur's accounting professional service establishments was brought about by a 1.53 percent in the number of accounting establishments operating from Kuala Lumpur. In percentage net income contributed by the Kuala Lumpur's accounting establishments towards the Kuala Lumpur's total net income, there was a reduction of 3.13 percent in ten years. In 1984, Kuala Lumpur's accounting establishments contributed 18.97 percent towards the Kuala Lumpur's total net income of RM91, 751,000, but in 1994, they contributed only 14.84 percent towards the Kuala Lumpur's total net income of RM1, 638,202,000.

The lawyers and surveyors service establishments, both showed positive changes in terms of percentage of establishments located in Kuala Lumpur and also percentage of net income contribution towards the total Malaysia's net income for the two professional service establishments. During the decade where data was available, there was a 2.31 percent change in percentage of legal establishments in Kuala Lumpur, from 32.05 percent (317 legal establishments) of 989 legal establishments in Malaysia in 1984 to 34.36 percent (633 legal establishments) of 1842 legal establishments in 1994. There was also a 7.19 percent improvement in net income contribution from the legal establishments in Kuala Lumpur towards the total Malaysia's legal establishments net income. In 1984, the Kuala Lumpur's legal establishments contributed 45.58 percent (RM29, 527,000) of the total net income for Malaysia's legal establishments of RM64, 777,000, while in 1994; it contributed 52.77 percent (RM409, 474,000) towards the total net income of Malaysia's legal establishments of RM775, 892,000. The percentage contribution from Kuala Lumpur's legal establishments towards the total net income for the Kuala Lumpur's six professional service establishments declined 7.18 percent in ten years. The Kuala Lumpur's legal establishments made the most contribution towards the Kuala Lumpur's total net income of RM91, 751,000 in 1984 (32.18 percent), whereas in 1994, the Kuala Lumpur's legal establishments' contribution was only 25.00 percent of the Kuala Lumpur's total net income of RM1, 638,202,000.

The case is slightly different for the Kuala Lumpur's surveyor establishments. The Kuala Lumpur's surveyors establishments' percentage contribution towards the Kuala Lumpur's total net income of RM91, 751,000 was 8.64 percent (RM7, 925,000) in 1984, whereas in 1994, the percentage contribution increased to 14.10 percent (RM231, 038,000) of the total Kuala Lumpur's net income of RM1, 638,202,000, (a 5.46 percent increase in ten years). In terms of percentage of establishments located in Kuala Lumpur, there was a 4.77 percent positive change, but in terms of percentage net income contribution from Kuala Lumpur's surveyor's establishments towards the Malaysia's surveyor's establishments' total net income, there was only a 1.79 percent change. In 1984, Kuala Lumpur had a 23.01 percent (78 establishments) share of the total 339 surveyors establishments in Malaysia, and the Kuala Lumpur's surveyor's establishments' of RM15, 482,000. A decade later, there were 125 surveyors establishments operating in Kuala Lumpur, which represented 27.78 percent (RM231, 038,000) towards the total net income for Malaysia's surveyors establishments of RM436, 091,000.

With respect to architectural establishments, Kuala Lumpur has 39.31 percent (125 establishments) of the total 318 architectural establishments in Malaysia, which contributed 53.80 percent (RM17, 753,000) towards the total net income for Malaysia's architectural establishments of RM32, 998,000. However, in 1994, the percentage of architectural establishments operating in Kuala Lumpur recorded a 0.69 percent drop to 38.62 percent (212 establishments) of the total 549 architectural establishments operating in Malaysia. The 212 architectural establishments in Kuala Lumpur contributed 55.66 percent (RM223, 995,000) towards the total net income for Malaysia's architectural establishments of RM402, 431,000. Thus, there was an increase of 1.86 percent in net income contributed by Kuala Lumpur's architectural establishments to Malaysia's total net income arising from the same activities despite the drop in percentage of architectural establishments operating in Kuala Lumpur. The data also shows that between 1984 through 1994, Kuala Lumpur's architectural establishments percentage contribution towards the total Kuala Lumpur's net income dropped by 5.68 percent. In 1984, the Kuala Lumpur's architectural establishments contributed 19.35 percent of the total Kuala Lumpur's net income of RM91, 751,000, but in 1994, Kuala Lumpur's architectural establishments contribute only 13.67 percent of the total Kuala Lumpur's net income of RM1, 638,202,000.

3.7. LOCATION OF PRODUCER SERVICES

Using information from the ***1998 Kuala Lumpur Yellow Pages*** it is possible to map the location of producer services establishments in Kuala Lumpur. Broadly, based on the patterns thus derived deductions as to the locational criteria and tendencies could be made.

From figures 3.1 to 3.5, some general locational tendencies among producer service activities are discernible. Producer service activities such as accountancy (Fig. 3.2), banks, insurance and finance companies (Fig. 3.3), secretarial and administrative services (Fig. 3.4), and legal services (Fig. 3.5) have tendencies to agglomerate in the city centre preferring all the advantages of a central city location. Arguably, the centrality of location of this group of producer services is explained by its ability to pay higher land and building rents. Centrality of location arise from the need to be accessible to other major economic activities and these could be other producer services establishments which are 'strategic' in nature and are often located in the central business district. With respect to banks, insurance and financial institutions, and legal services, Clark's (1951) decreasing density function seems to apply: as distance increases from the city centre of Kuala Lumpur, the intensity or incidence of these activities tends to decrease. This density function is visible along the main urban development axes leading from the centre such as Jalan Syed Putra and Jalan Bangsar.

While there are observable concentration tendencies in the city centre and other business centres around the city (Taman Tun Dr Ismail and Bukit Damansara) and along main arterial routes such as Jalan Bangsar and Jalan Syed Putra, generally other producer service activities as noted in Figure 3.1 tend to spread all over the city. These producer service activities could be categorized as the 'footloose' type and they tend to progressively spread out to new growth areas or along newly developed routes without reference to any specific locational criteria. This is the common explanation for the locational tendency for this group of services. On a much closer look this may not be entirely the case. It seems, on one hand, that some producer service establishments are pursuing a strategy whereby they aimed at enlarging their markets. On the other hand, there is a pull factor operating. Evidently there are significantly increased demands in outer areas of the city in particular in new residential and industrial growth areas. The interactive nature of producer service activities makes accessibility a primary factor for locational choice: proximity between supply and demand may in several cases represent a competitive advantage.

Figure 3.1:Spatial Distribution of Service Establishments in Kuala Lumpur, 1998 (Miscellaneous Services)

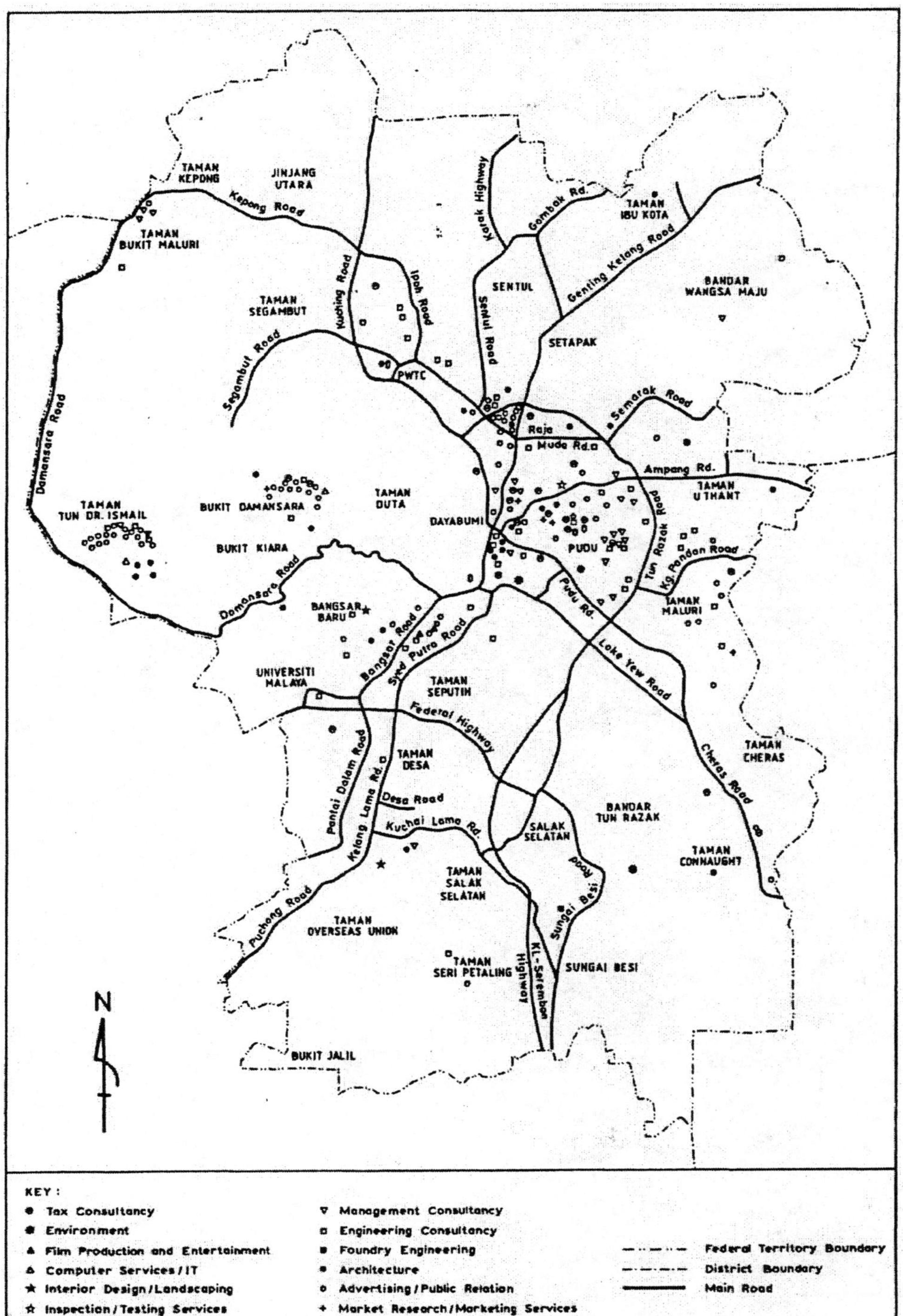

Figure 3.2: Spatial Distribution of Service Establishments in Kuala Lumpur, 1998 (Telecommunication, Real Estate, and Accounting Services)

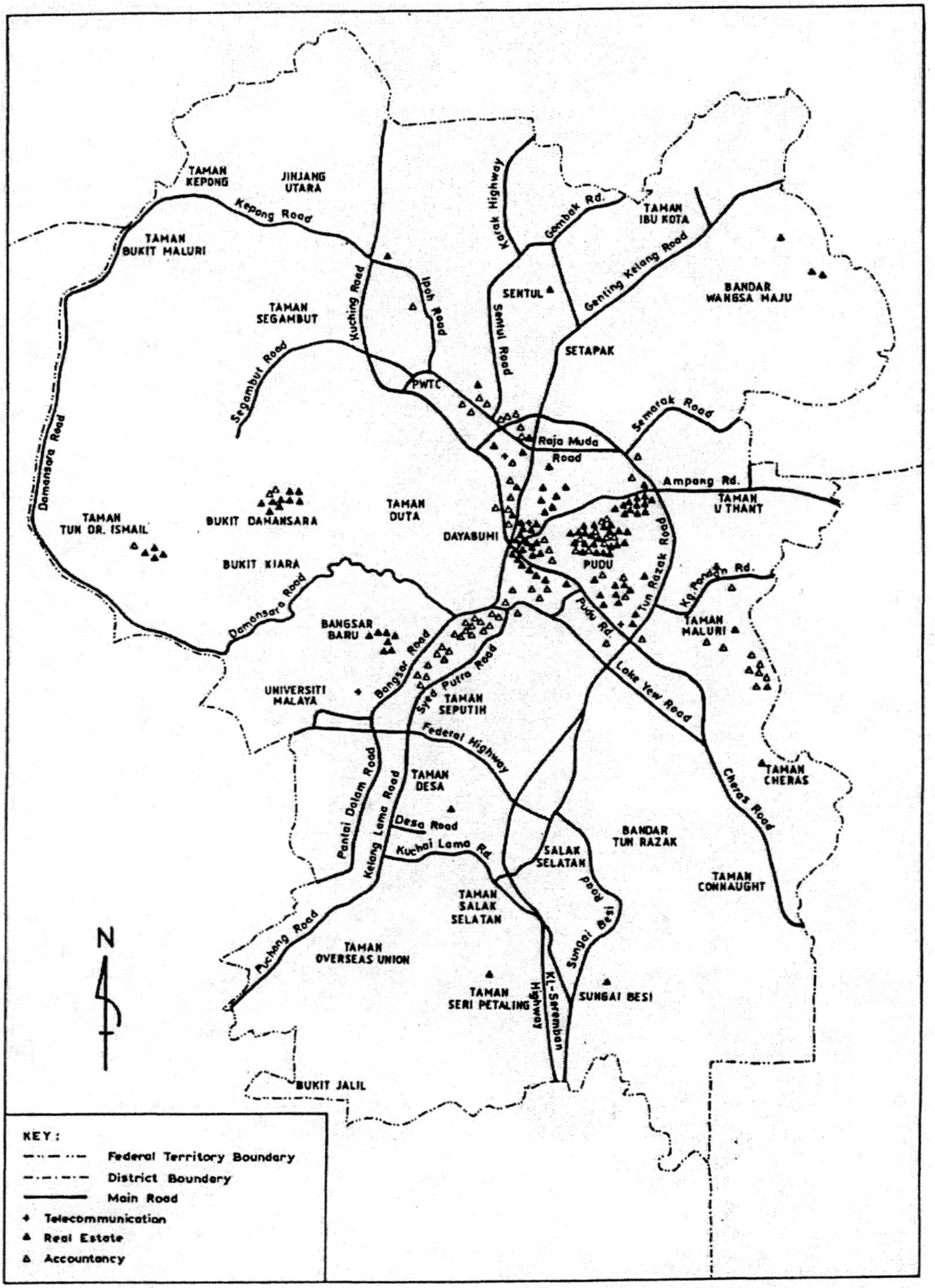

Figure 3.3: Spatial Distribution of Service Establishments in Kuala Lumpur, 1998 (Banking, Insurance and Finance Services)

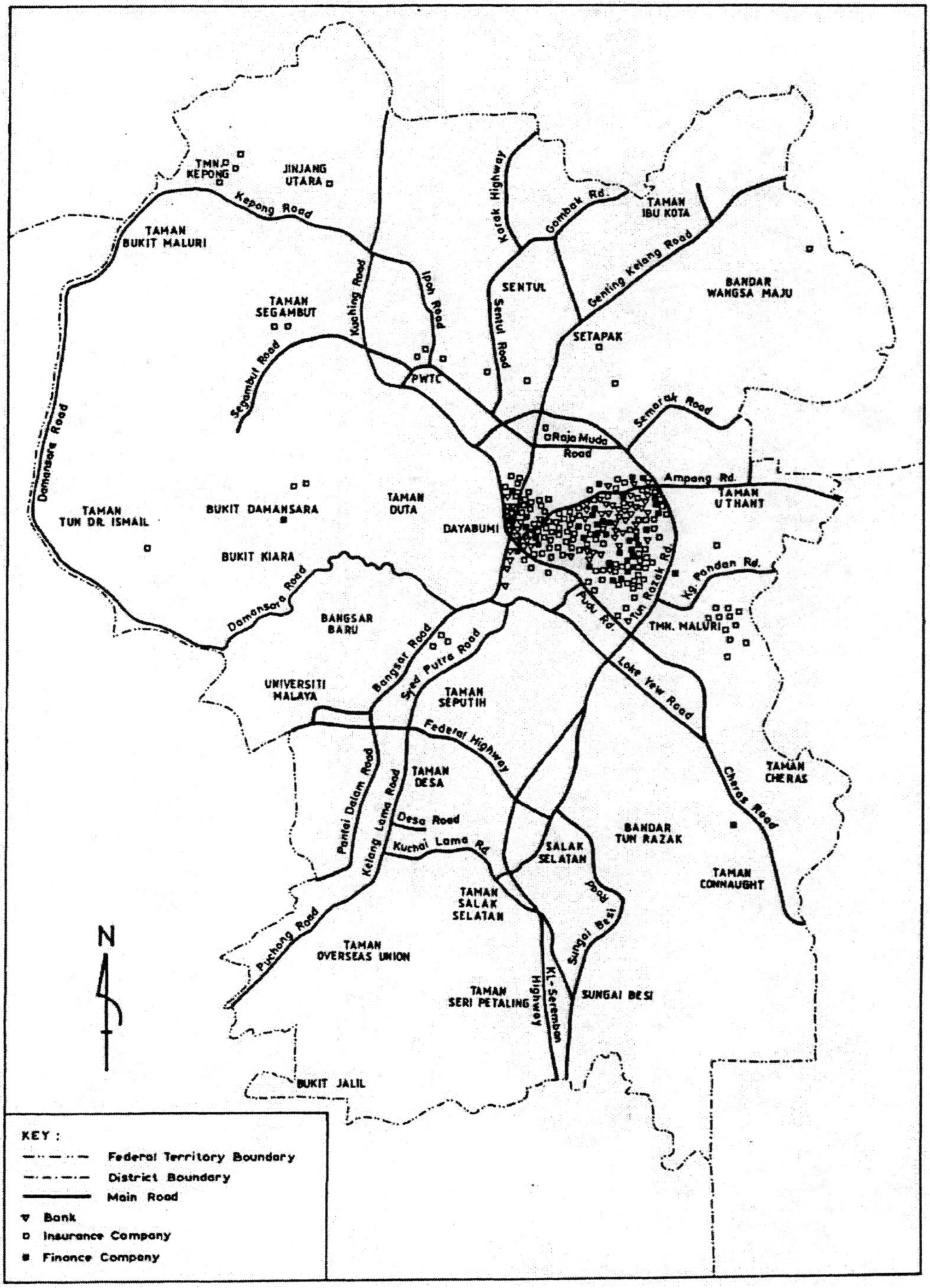

Figure 3.4: Spatial Distribution of Service Establishments in Kuala Lumpur, 1998 (Recruitment/Employment and Secretarial/Administrative Services)

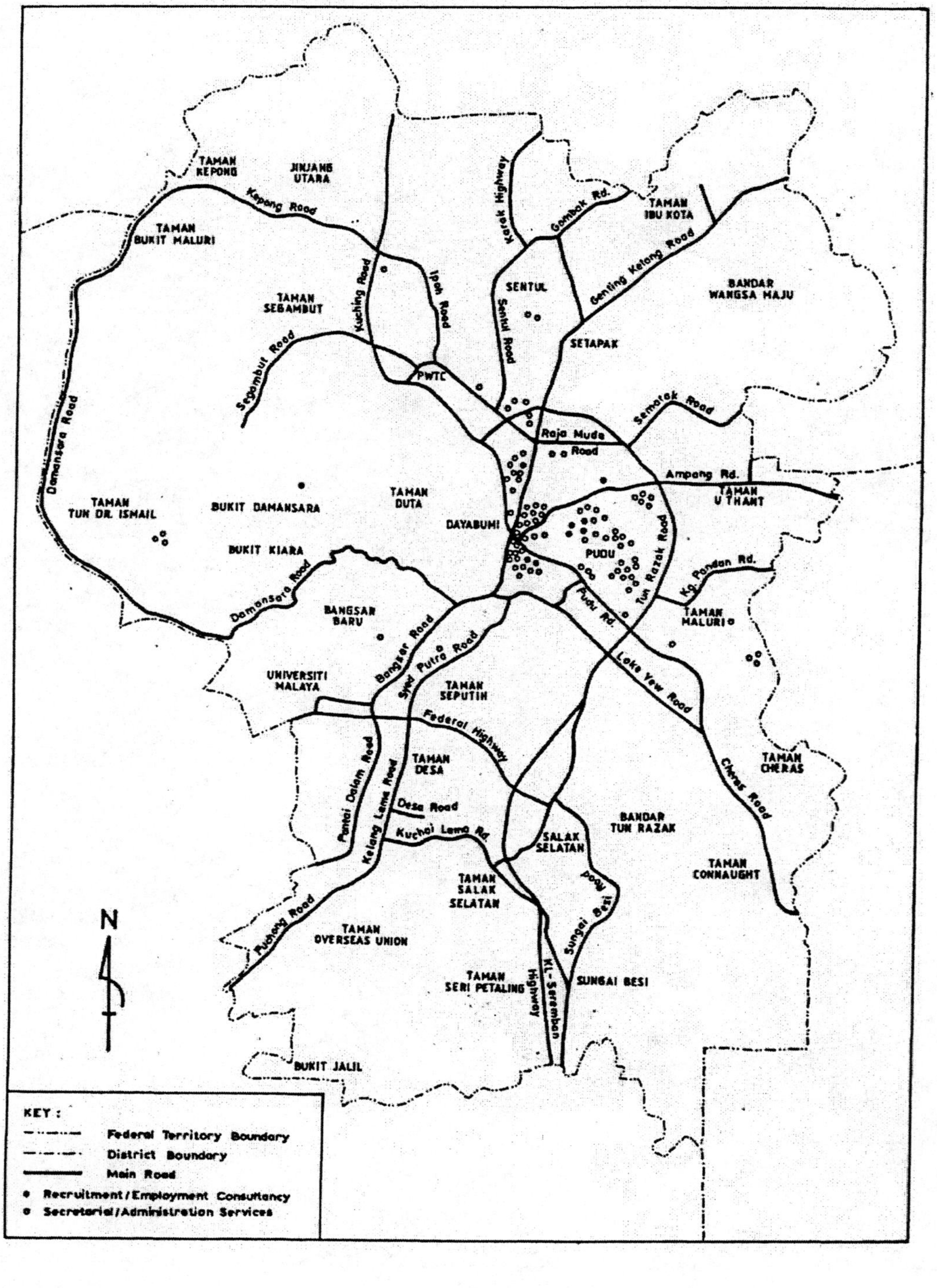

Figure 3.5: Spatial Distribution of Service Establishments in Kuala Lumpur, 1998 (Legal Services)

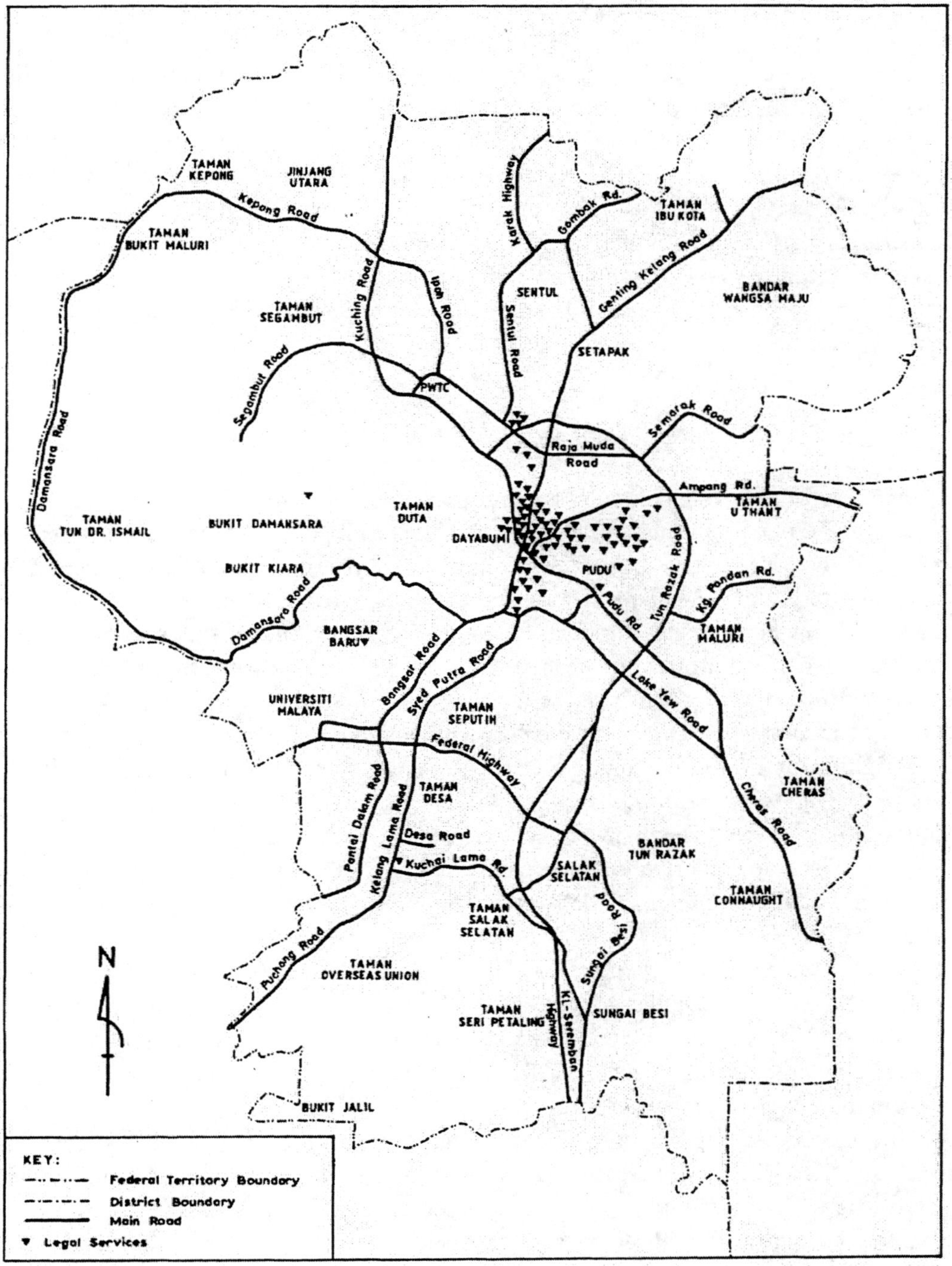

On examining the spatial patterns and locational tendencies of service establishments it appears that rapid growth of producer services in particular have resulted in internal social and spatial organization of Kuala Lumpur. Much have been said about the changes to the fabric of Kuala Lumpur, in particular its city centre as a result of expansion in service sector and other related development (see Morshidi and Suriati, 1999). But what is very evident of late is the transformation of the relationship between the Golden Triangle Area for instance with the periphery to the south of the city. Because of the emergence of centres of economic activity (and many more in the pipe-line) in the immediate periphery of the city 'footloose' service industries have located themselves around office parks, and science or technological park. But these new developments in the periphery are not in any way competing with the highly specialized functions of the CBD. But it has to be emphasized that the present development is attributable to government policy as it is due to the location and relocation of some categories of the service sector.

3.8. Discussion and Conclusion

The service sector, in particular the producer component of it, plays an important role in the life and development of cities such as Kuala Lumpur. Producer services activities have very powerful effects on cities based on the fact that they do initiate centripetal and centrifugal tendencies among other related activities. At the level of a city the size of Kuala Lumpur it is quite possible to gauge just how much the service sector is contributing to urban growth and change. This will be the subject matter of Chapter 4. An indication of the thriving nature of the service sector in Kuala Lumpur is provided by the amount of income contributed and employment generated. These have been shown to be quite significant in Kuala Lumpur. It is also possible to pinpoint where growth are occurring. But what has not been established empirically here is the extent of the relationship between growth in service sector activities and urban policy initiatives. However, based on cursory observation and readings of the trend in urban strategies such relationship could be inferred. Indeed other studies have shown this to be (see Morshidi and Suriati, 1999).

In conclusion, this chapter has highlighted the impacts of the economic transformation from manufacturing to services (analysed earlier in Chapter 2) on the economy of Kuala Lumpur. Recent major growth in services, in particular producer services, has brought the question of the important role of this sub-sector in the urban economy of a rapidly globalizing city. Evidently, not all categories of the service sector have been contributing positively and in large proportion to the city's economy. Nonetheless, collectively, increased activity and contribution of expanding and growing activities is undoubtedly both critical and essential to the future growth of the Kuala Lumpur's economy. It was noted also the fact that the shift from manufacturing to services have some important spatial and locational impacts. There are obvious policy implications arising from this shift. Evidently, certain high-order producer services tend to centralise in the city centre and once again proved that certain service activities are biased in their locational choices. Banking, finance, insurance, and legal services are strongly attracted to the city centre as a result of increasing tertiarization of the city centre economy and the steep increase in land values. Engineering consultancies, scientific laboratories and other manufacturing-related services are attracted to the immediate periphery and other new industrial and residential areas outside the limits of the city centre, where their main clients have meanwhile moved, following a desuburbanization and metropolitan expansion process of the city of Kuala Lumpur. Diffusion to the periphery carries with it other activities, which are complementary to their own. It has to be noted that this transformation to services in Kuala Lumpur is indicative of a significant modification in the production system in the city.

Chapter 4

SELECTED SERVICE ACTIVITIES IN KUALA LUMPUR: AGGREGATE DATA ANALYSIS

4.1. INTRODUCTION

The purpose of this chapter is to present the result of an in-depth analysis of aggregate data for service activities in Kuala Lumpur. The main data source for this chapter is the unpublished data from ***Census of Selected Service Industries, 1992*** and ***Census of Professional and Institutional Establishments (Private Sector), 1994.*** At the time of writing this report the unpublished data for ***Census of Selected Service Industries, 1997*** and ***Census of Professional and Institutional Establishments (Private Sector), 1997*** were not available for analysis. For this limitation it was not possible to show the dynamics of the service sector in Kuala Lumpur. This chapter therefore will only examine and analyse in greater detail the performances of the accountancy and advertising establishments in 1994 in order to unravel their specific performance with a view to determining growth potentials and contribution to the economy of Kuala Lumpur. These two service activities were selected for detailed analysis, as they are distinctively producer service activities. Based on the two censuses noted above, it is not possible to determine whether other service activities could easily be classified as producer services for they clearly served final consumers too.

Performance of accountancy and advertising establishments will be analysed in terms of the following broad categories on the basis of per establishments or per employee. These broad categories are as follows:

- revenue
- expenditure
- employment generation,
- salaries and wages paid,
- value of fixed assets owned

Performance criteria, on the other hand, will be analysed in relation to the organisational characteristics of the service establishments. The following organizational characteristics are chosen:

- legal status
- ownership
- revenue size group
- fixed assets size
- total employment size

4.2. ACCOUNTANCY ESTABLISHMENTS: PERFORMANCE IN 1994

4.2.1 Principal Statistics and Performance by Legal Status and Ownership, 1994 – Kuala Lumpur

In 1994, there were a total of 305 accounting establishments in Kuala Lumpur, of which 304 were Malaysian residents-owned. Of this 304, 211 establishments or 69.2 percent were classified as individual proprietorship, 77 or 25.3 percent were partnership and 16 or 5.3 percent were private limited establishments.

In terms of performance, from Table 4.1, establishments operating under partnership arrangement generated an average of RM 2,578,590 per establishment. Interestingly, private limited establishments, which generated less revenue than those operating under individual proprietorship, actually generated more revenue per establishment.

Establishments operating under partnership arrangement recorded the highest profit (RM 42,893,000), followed by establishments in the proprietorship category (RM 12,425,000) (Table 4.1). Overall, the table suggested that all the establishments were making profits.

On average, the partnership establishments hired 60 employees per establishment (Table 4.1). Although the individual proprietorship establishments hired 2,030 workers compared to private limited establishments, which hired 178 workers, both, had the same number of employees per establishment.

The partnership establishments reported higher salary per worker (Table 4. 1). From the same table it can also be seen that they reported higher revenue per employee, which meant higher worker's productivity. In addition, all of these groups spent an amount close to 50 percent of their expenditure on salaries and wages alone. (Table 4.1). Therefore labor is a very important component to this sector.

However, on average, it was the partnership establishments that owned the highest amount of fixed assets per establishment. Followed by the private limited establishments and the individual proprietorship establishments (Table 4.1).

Table 4.1 Accountancy establishments in Kuala Lumpur: performance by legal status and ownership, 1994

Legal Status	Revenue per establishment (RM' 000)	Profit/loss margin (RM' 000)	Employee per establishment (RM' 000)	Salary per worker (RM' 000)	Revenue per employee (RM' 000)	Percentage of salary and wages paid to expenditure (%)	Fixed Assets per establishment (RM' 000)
Individual Proprietorship							
Malaysian Residents (211)	239.90	12,425	10	10.76	24.93	51.07	56.99
Partnership							
Malaysian Residents and Joint Ownership (78)	2,578.59	42,893	59	20.50	43.62	56.93	117.99
Private Limited							
Malaysian Residents (16)	408.38	258	11	17.02	36.70	48.30	72.38

Source Department of Statistics, Malaysia. 1994. Census of Selected Service Industries, 1992 (Unpublished data)

4.2.2 Principal Statistics and Performance by Ownership and Revenue Size Group, 1994 – Kuala Lumpur

A significant majority of Malaysian residents-owned accountancy establishments fall under the small to medium revenue size group. In terms of performance, establishments reporting revenue of RM 500,000 to less than RM 1,000,000 generated higher average revenue than those that fall within the RM 200,000 to less than RM 500,000 revenue size group (Table 4.2). From table 4.2, it can be seen that all establishments, irrespective of revenue size group, made some amount of profits and the highest (RM28, 022,000) being reported from establishments with revenue of RM 5,000,000 and more.

Establishments reporting revenue of RM 5,000,000 and more performed rather well in terms of employment generated per establishment (employing well above 100 employees per establishment). Establishments reporting revenue of between RM 200,000 to less than RM 5,000,000 hired, on average, less than 100 employees.

On average, there appears to be a relationship between the size of the establishments, measured in terms of revenue, and the amount of salary per worker (Table 4.2). The RSG of RM 5,000,000 and more reported paying the highest average salary and the RSG of less than RM 20,000 paid the lowest salary per worker.

If revenue per employee is used as an indicator of worker's productivity, then the establishments, which paid higher average salary, experienced higher worker's productivity. In addition, from table 4.2, labor is very important to establishments with large revenue because they spend almost half of their expenditure on salaries and wages. For instance, the percentage of salaries and wages paid as component of expenditure by the establishments with revenue of RM 100,000 and more was close to 50 percent.

Fixed assets per establishment tend to increase with the revenue size of establishments. Establishments with revenue exceeding RM 5,000,000 have accumulated substantial assets.

4.2.3 Principal Statistics and Performance by Ownership and Total Employment Size Group, 1994 – Kuala Lumpur

Locally owned establishments tend to be small in terms of the number of employees. Evidently, a substantial majority tends to have less than twenty employees. Performance wise, there appears to be a connection between establishments' employment size with revenue. Revenue seems to be determined labor intensity of the establishments concerned (Table 4.3).

In terms of salary per worker, there appears to be a connection between higher average salary paid and the size of the establishments, as measured by number of employees (Table 4.3). It is interesting to note that establishments with less than 5 employees could command comparatively higher revenue per employee. For this group of establishments salaries and wages accounted for less than 25 percent of their expenditures. They may be investing on equipment and other productivity increasing measures.

Table 4.2 Accountancy establishments in Kuala Lumpur: performance by ownership and revenue size group, 1994

REVENUE SIZE GROUP	Revenue per establishment (RM' 000)	Profit/loss margin (RM' 000)	Employee per establishment (RM' 000)	Salary per worker (RM' 000)	Revenue per employee (RM' 000)	Percentage of salary and wages paid to expenditure %	Fixed assets per establishment (RM' 000)
Malaysian Residents							
Less than 20,000 (9)	7.50	20	2	2.50	4.53	31.25	1.00
20,000 - < 50,000 (30)	33.90	158	3	6.35	13.56	27.36	16.97
50,000 - < 100,000 (27)	74.56	476	4	7.75	16.92	44.37	13.85
100,000 < 200,000 (66)	148.58	2,627	8	9.68	23.52	46.54	44.52
200,000 - < 500,000 (105)	313.82	8,164	13	10.62	25.09	51.56	77.32
500,000 - < 1,000,000 (39)	652.61	5,017	25	11.60	26.32	51.48	86.18
1,000,000 - < 5,000,000 (22)	1,891.77	11,092	55	15.70	34.48	59.61	82.50
5,000,000 and more *(includes one firm of joint ownership) (7)	20,764.40	28,022	387	25.31	53.71	56.97	751.57

Source: Department of Statistics, Malaysia. 1994. Census of Selected Service Industries.1992 (Unpublished Data)

Table 4.3 Accountancy establishments in Kuala Lumpur: performance by ownership and total employment size group, 1994.

Total Employment Size Group	Revenue per establishment (RM' 000)	Profit/loss margin (RM' 000)	Employee per establishment (RM' 000)	Salary per worker (RM' 000)	Revenue per employee (RM' 000)	Percentage of salary and wages paid to expenditure (%)	Fixed Assets per establishment (RM' 000)
Malaysian Resident							
Less than 5 (79)	111.65	2,650	3	12.81	42.81	24.29	18.72
5 - 9 (82)	177.24	4,122	7	10.69	26.33	47.11	44.88
10 - 19 (84)	363.23	7,019	14	11.28	26.23	51.29	68.96
20 - 29 (24)	650.17	4,094	23	12.11	28.22	54.75	141.58
30 - 49 (14)	940.14	2,556	36	12.96	26.27	58.17	118.93
50 - 99 (12)	1,496.67	4,255	62	12.56	24.30	65.53	57.08
100 - 199 (3)	4,111.67	2,859	133	15.04	30.91	61.90	141.33
200 and more *(includes one firm of joint ownership) (7)	20,764.43	28,021	387	25.31	53.71	56.97	751.72

Source: Department of Statistics, Malaysia. 1994. Census of Selected Service Industries, 1992 (Unpublished Data)

4.2.4 Principal Statistics and Performance by Ownership and Fixed Assets Size Group, 1994 – Kuala Lumpur

No less than 2/3 of the 305 accounting establishments in Kuala Lumpur owned fixed assets amounting to less than RM 50,000. In fact 66 percent of establishments have less than RM 10,000 worth of fixed assets.

Table 4.4 summarizes the performance of accountancy establishments on various measures. Establishments with fixed assets of between RM 500,000 to less than RM 5,000,000 performed rather well with high average revenue per establishment.

From table 4.4, it can be seen that all establishments with less than RM500, 000 worth of fixed assets had less than 100 employees per establishment whereas those with less than RM100, 000 worth of fixed assets had 20 or less employees. Only establishments with assets worth between RM500, 000 to less than RM5, 000,000 had 267 employees per establishment.

Establishments with low fixed assets (e.g. less than RM10, 000) paid a high per worker salary compared with establishments with between RM100, 000 to less than RM200, 000 worth of assets. The later only paid a salary of RM10, 930 per employee. As for employees' productivity, establishments, which offer the highest salary per worker, also had the highest labour productivity.

4.3. Advertising Establishments: Performance in 1994

4.3.1 Principal Statistics and Performance by Legal Status and Ownership, 1994

There were a total of 66 advertising establishments in Kuala Lumpur in 1994. Of this, 59 or 89 percent were Malaysian residents-owned. Again of the 66 establishments, 61 or 92 percent were classified as private limited. All 7 non-Malaysian-owned establishments were legally instituted as private limited operation.

Private Limited establishments under Malaysian ownership generated the highest number of employment as compared to the other categories of advertising establishments. Although the non-Malaysian residents establishments hired a total of 379 employees as compared to 1,838 hired by Malaysian residents establishments, they had on average 54 employees per establishment, which is higher than the 34 employees per establishment hired by Malaysian Residents establishments. Labour productivity per employee of the non-Malaysian residents establishments of RM532, 820 was significantly higher than that of Malaysian-owned establishments. (Table 4.5)

Table 4.4 Accountancy establishments in Kuala Lumpur: performance by ownership and fixed assets size group, 1994.

Fixed Assets Size Group	Revenue per establishment (RM' 000)	Profit/loss margin (RM' 000)	Employee per establishment (RM' 000)	Salary per worker (RM' 000)	Revenue per employee (RM' 000)	Percentage of salary and wages paid to expenditure %	Fixed Assets per establishment (RM' 000)
Malaysian Residents							
Less than 10,000 (85)	559.55	9,989	12	22.57	52.72	54.18	2.90
10,000 - < 20,000 (33)	240.24	2,320	8	11.72	28.52	50.16	15.30
20,000 - < 50,000 (84)	338.15	6,911	13	12.09	26.67	54.14	34.14
50,000 - < 100,000 (49)	552.08	6,991	20	11.99	27.30	55.34	72.00
100,000 - < 200,000 (29)	573.24	3,909	23	10.93	24.89	54.76	139.48
200,000 - < 500,000 (20)	3,197.95	16,589	73	21.92	43.81	64.93	293.20
500,000 - < 5,000,000 *(includes one joint ownership firm) (5)	13,349.4	8,867	267	22.02	50.04	50.08	1,065.80

Source: Department of Statistics, Malaysia. 1994. Census of Selected Service Industries, 1992 (Unpublished data)

Table 4.5 Advertising establishments in Kuala Lumpur: performance by ownership and legal status, 1994

Legal Status	Revenue per establishment (RM'000)	Profit/loss margin (RM'000)	Employee per establishments	Salary per worker (RM'000)	Revenue per employee (RM'000)	Percentage of Salary and Wages paid to Expenditure (%)	Fixed Assets per establishment *(RM'000)*
Malaysian Residents							
Individual Proprietorship & Partnership (5)	452.4	+154	9	6.74	52.60	12.14	52.20
Private Limited (54)	11,966.63	+10,389	34	34.30	351.58	9.92	521.61
Non-Malaysian Residents							
Private Limited (7)	28,848.57	+3,505	54	46.84	532.82	8.95	464.57

Source: Department of Statistics, Malaysia. 1994. Census of Selected Service Industries, 1992 (Unpublished data)

4.3.2. Principal Statistics and Performance by Ownership and Revenue Size Group, 1994 – Kuala Lumpur

Ninety-three percent of Malaysian residents owned establishments falling within the RM200, 000 to less than RM30 million revenue size group (Table 4.6). Of the 7 non-Malaysian-owned establishments two are considerably larger and fall within the RM100 million and above revenue size group.

Establishments under Malaysian ownership generated revenue totaling RM648, 551,000, and the single largest contribution (37.12 percent) came from establishments under the RM30, 000,000 - less than RM200, 000,000 group. This group also generated more revenue than all non-Malaysian owned establishments combined.

Establishments under Malaysian ownership spent RM637, 917,000. No less than 38 percent of this expenditure comes from establishments with larger revenue based (RM30, 000,000 to less than RM200, 000,000). Establishments controlled by non-Malaysian of the category RM1, 000,000 - less than RM100, 000,000 was the largest single factor in total expenditure for non-Malaysian establishments.

Performances of advertising establishments are listed in Table 4.6. Evidently, advertising activities could be considered as profitable venture for most establishments, except for those in the RM15, 000,000 - < RM20, 000,000 revenue size group. This group reported losses of RM889, 000. Establishments in the RM30, 000,000 to less than RM200, 000,000 revenue size group reported substantial revenue and considerable value added. Again, establishments in the RM30, 000,000 - < RM200, 000,000 revenue size group and under local ownership reported high labor productivity.

Evidently, the smaller the establishments in terms of revenue, the higher are the proportion of their expenditure for salary and accumulation of fixed assets. For larger establishments (in terms of revenue), the proportion of expenditure for salary and wages and accumulation of fixed assets tend to be lower. The evident seems to suggest that loss making establishments spent more of their revenue on labour.

4.3.3 Principal Statistics and Performance by Ownership and Total Employment Size Group, 1994 – Kuala Lumpur

Among Malaysian controlled advertising establishments, 76 percent have less than 50 employees (Table 4.7). Five out of 7 foreign-controlled establishments were considerably larger in terms of number of employees (more than 50).

Table 4.6 Advertising establishments in Kuala Lumpur: performance by ownership and revenue size group, 1994

Revenue Size Group	Revenue per establishment (RM'000)	Profit/loss margin (RM'000)	Employee per establishments	Salary per worker (RM'000)	Revenue per employee (RM'000)	Percentage of Salary and Wages paid to Expenditure (%)	Fixed Assets per establishment *(RM'000)*
Malaysian Residents							
100 - < 500 (10)	343.4	+ 208	7	12.57	51.25	24.55	46.10
500 - < 1,000 (7)	867.6	+ 209	10	15.19	83.19	18.66	105.86
1,000 - < 5,000 (16)	2,817.7	+ 1,538	22	17.39	130.30	14.02	410.44
5,000 - < 10,000 (8)	8,082.4	+ 2,174	53	35.25	151.43	24.09	831.50
10,000 - < 15,000 (8)	11,951.4	+ 2,293	39	23.12	310.43	7.63	825.13
15,000 - < 20,000 (3)	16,569.0	- 889	53	42.92	310.67	13.57	538.67
20,000 - < 30,000 (3)	22,744.0	+ 637	44	44.12	513.02	8.68	89.67
30,000 - < 200,000 (4)	78,915.3	+4,373	92	55.59	860.11	6.55	774.25
Non-Malaysian Residents							
1,000 - < 100,000 (12)	28,848.6	+ 3,505	54	46.84	532.82	8.95	464.57

Source: Department of Statistics, Malaysia. 1994. Census of Selected Service Industries, 1992 (Unpublished data)

In terms of revenue, the largest revenue earners were Malaysian-controlled establishments, in particular those with between 50 and 200 employees. This group of establishments contributed to no less than 49.31 percent of total revenue from this sub-sector in 1994. Small establishments (less than 5 employees) were insignificant contributors to total revenue (0.12 percent of total revenue). From table 4.6, Malaysian-controlled establishments in the 50 to less than 200 employees collected total revenue of RM29, 950,210, the highest revenue per establishment. Non-Malaysian controlled establishments, in particular those in the 10 to less than 100 employees category, earned RM28, 848,570 per establishment. However it should be noted that there were 14 Malaysian establishments and 7 in the non-Malaysian category.

Larger establishments tend to make up a larger proportion of total expenditure. Almost 50 percent of total expenditure incurred by advertising establishments came from the 50 to 200-employee category. For the foreign-controlled establishments, establishments in the 10 to 100-employee category spend RM198, 435,000 or 23.73 percent of total expenditure.

From table 4.6, Malaysian-controlled establishments in the 50 to 200-employee category reported the highest profit. Evidently, although Malaysian establishments in the 30 to 50-employee category generated less revenue compared to non-Malaysian establishments, their profits margin of about RM3, 007,000 was only marginally lower than that of non-Malaysian controlled establishments.

In terms of impact on salary and wage pattern, almost 54 percent of total salaries and wages were incurred by Malaysian establishments in the 50 to 200-employee group. For establishments under Non-Malaysian Residents ownership, almost 22 percent of salaries and wages came from those in the 10 to 100-employee category spend 21.90 percent of total salaries and wages paid.

For Malaysian-controlled establishments, those with between 30 to 200 employees owned no less than 62 percent of total fixed assets. The pattern among non-Malaysian establishments is quite similar, with the larger ones having larger fixed assets.

4.3.4 Principal Statistics and Performance by Ownership and Fixed Assets Size Group, 1994 – Kuala Lumpur

Of the 59 establishments under Malaysian ownership, 20 or 34 percent fall in the 'RM50, 000-100,000' category; 56 percent have sizeable assets of more than RM2000, 000. Establishments under non-Malaysian ownership tend to be of 'more than RM100, 000' worth of fixed assets.

Performance-wise, Malaysian-controlled establishments in the RM200, 000 to RM5, 000,000 generated a substantial proportion (no less than 71 percent) to total revenues compared to those with smaller fixed assets. Similarly, among foreign-controlled establishments, those with more than RM500, 000 fixed assets contributed substantial proportion to total revenue.

Table 4.7 Advertising establishments in Kuala Lumpur: performance by ownership and total employment size group, 1994

Total Employment Size Group	Revenue per Establishment (RM'000)	Profit/Loss Margin (RM'000)	Number of Employees per Establishments	Salary per Employee (RM'000)	Revenue per Employee *(RM'000)*	Percentage of Salary and Wages paid to Expenditure (%)	Fixed Assets per Establishment (RM'000)
Malaysian Residents							
Less than 5 (4)	254.75	+ 55	2	11.43	127.38	8.30	22.25
5 - < 10 (13)	892.38	+ 620	7	19.44	119.60	16.82	103.46
10 - < 20 (9)	3,048.44	+ 368	15	16.06	207.85	7.83	91.78
20 - < 30 (8)	4,850.25	+ 1,158	24	19.60	204.22	9.79	798.38
30 - < 50 (11)	13,663.55	+ 3,007	38	29.09	357.85	8.30	688.36
50 - < 200 (14)	29,950.21	+ 5,335	74	41.83	405.52	10.47	872.07
Non-Malaysian Residents							
10 - < 100 (7)	28,848.57	+ 3,505	54	46.84	532.82	8.95	464.57

Source: Department of Statistics, Malaysia. 1994. Census of Selected Service Industries, 1992 (Unpublished data)

Table 4.8 Advertising establishments in Kuala Lumpur: performance by ownership and fixed assets size group, 1994

Fixed Assets Size Group (RM'000)	Revenue per establishment (RM'000)	Profit/loss margin (RM'000)	Employee per establishment	Salary per worker (RM'000)	Revenue per employee (RM'000)	Percentage of Salary and Wages paid to Expenditure (%)	Fixed Assets per establishment (RM'000)
Malaysian Residents							
Less than 20 (3)	1,269.00	- 435	6	13.50	211.50	5.73	7.33
20 - < 50 (10)	1,152.90	+ 538	9	16.77	134.06	12.60	31.30
50 - < 100 (10)	2,162.50	+ 725	13	14.13	162.59	8.79	74.40
100 - < 200 (3)	3,930.33	+ 313	18	20.11	214.38	9.64	143.00
200 - < 500 (16)	9,545.88	+ 4,181	35	24.66	273.23	9.28	310.44
500 - < 1,000 (8)	39,179.25	+ 2,566	66	43.66	597.02	7.37	629.00
1,000 - < 5,000 (9)	14,837.89	+ 2,655	56	43.60	264.44	16.82	1,880.11
Non-Malaysian Residents							
20 - < 500	26,938.00	+ 1,319	43	52.25	621.65	8.54	159.67
500 - < 1,000	30,281.25	+ 2,187	62	44.01	486.45	921	693.25

Source: Department of Statistics, Malaysia. 1994. Census of Selected Service Industries, 1992 (Unpublished data)

From table 4.8, establishments in the 'RM500, 000 to less than RM1 million' group and under Malaysian-controlled reported high revenue per establishment (about RM39.2 million each). Malaysian-owned establishments of the category 'RM20, 000 to less than RM50, 000' earned the least, about RM1.15 million per establishment.

Establishments within the 'RM200, 000 to less than RM500, 000' group tend to report high profit margin. Most establishments reported a positive profit margin except for Malaysian-owned establishments in the category 'less than RM20, 000'.

Establishments of significantly higher fixed assets tend to employ significantly more workers. For instance, Malaysian-owned establishments with fixed assets of more than RM 200,000 employed 84 percent of the total 1881 employees in this sub-sector.

Malaysian establishments with more than RM200, 000 fixed assets accounted for 44.2 percent of total payment for salaries and wages worth RM63, 303 million. Similarly, among non-Malaysian establishments, those with considerably more fixed assets paid out more in terms of salaries and wages.

4.4 CONCLUSION

The accountancy and advertising establishments in Kuala Lumpur have shown great potential in the early nineties. On average and on the basis of per establishment these two types of producer services activities have fared better. From the evidence presented it is not quite true that foreign controlled establishments performed any better than locally owned establishments at least with respect to accountancy and advertising establishments

Accountancy and advertising services are generally thought to be dominated by foreign controlled organizations, but this is not quite the case. Locally controlled establishments have been shown to have significant share in the market for the services in Kuala Lumpur.

Chapter 5

PROFILES OF PRODUCER SERVICES ESTABLISHMENTS SURVEYED

5.1. INTRODUCTION

In order to assess the role and contributions of producer services sector in urban development it is imperative that we isolate the 'typical' establishments in terms of various characteristics. What specific characteristics are associated with variations in export performance, for example? Typically, in many studies, an analysis on the basis of a matched-pairs framework to control firm size, age and nature of service (i.e. factors expected to influence performance) was carried out (see for example, O'Farrell and Hitchens, 1988). Arguably, because Kuala Lumpur is also Malaysia's capital and its largest city, it was shown in earlier chapters that the city has the most extensive range of establishments within the producer services sector. This diversification also involves markets, labour usage, trade patterns, locational patterns and organizational structures. It was also shown that Kuala Lumpur has been experiencing spectacular growth in producer services in the last few years. Undoubtedly, various producer services segments have contributed to this growth. This chapter introduces some salient features of the surveyed establishments. These characteristics will be examined again in later chapters in relation to specific performance criteria in order to assess their role in the context of the urban development of Kuala Lumpur. From such an exercise, policy prescriptions can be generated and subsequently evaluated.

5.2. SURVEYED ESTABLISHMENTS' CHARACTERISTICS

Figure 5.1 shows the location of surveyed establishments. A high proportion of the sampled establishments are located in the city centre, reflecting the fact that producer service activities have a tendency to be centrally located. Table 5.1 shows the characteristics of the surveyed establishments. Out of the total sample, 81.5 percent of establishments were independent and locally owned, comprising of 52.2 percent single-site and 29.3 percent multi-site operations. Of the multi-site establishments, 34.8 percent had their headquarters in Kuala Lumpur, 2.2 percent in Chicago, and 2.2 percent in Europe. At least 30.0 percent have branches all over the country and also the Asian region while 3.3 percent have branches worldwide. 74.0 percent of respondent establishments (single and multi-site) agreed that 'network' (multi-site) is a form of spatial organization that would enable establishments concerned to maintain close relationship with the Kuala Lumpur markets, while at the same time hoping to serve a broader market area. An equally large majority of both single and multi-site operations (63.0 percent) believed that network is essential since this organizational form helps to increase market shares, reduce expenditures, and facilitate the mobility of the labour force. A little over 50.0 percent of respondents thought that for many services activities a network is the only way to gain access to substantial economies of scale offered by the Kuala Lumpur urban economy. Interestingly, for some 34.8 percent of networked establishments, their locational characteristics highlight their elementary status because their branches and headquarters are located within Kuala Lumpur.

The fact that a majority of the surveyed establishments are independent, single-site and locally-owned, it is inevitable that organizational set-up in the form of 'network' is less frequently adopted. Arguably, not all establishments are capable of implementing network strategy, and not all activities lend themselves to it with the same ease (see also, Leo and Philippe, 1991). These establishments are essentially 'compact' in nature and the small establishment size (less than 25 employees) of the sample in Kuala Lumpur confirms this fact.

In the case of the networked establishments, separation or division of tasks between the headquarters/office and the branch establishments is not very clear. Analysis of dominant activities highlights this situation. This analysis reveals that, among the networked establishments, monoactivity is not common. Different establishments were being formed in order to enable simultaneous presence of administration and marketing personnel. The branch establishments appear to be both the place of work for personnel and the point of sale of the services. Sales networks among the surveyed establishments typically involve activities where service is directly provided to clients.

It has to be noted that some establishments, in particular advertising, accounting and management consultancy, subsidiaries in Kuala Lumpur are clearly independent of their parent conglomerates. This type of legal structure or relationship is adopted in order to enable establishments located in Kuala Lumpur diversify service activities. Each establishment is autonomous in terms of management and administration, and it carries out its own local marketing policy, which appears to be efficient.

Figure 5.1: Spatial Distribution of the 92 Surveyed Producer Service Establishments In Kuala Lumpur.

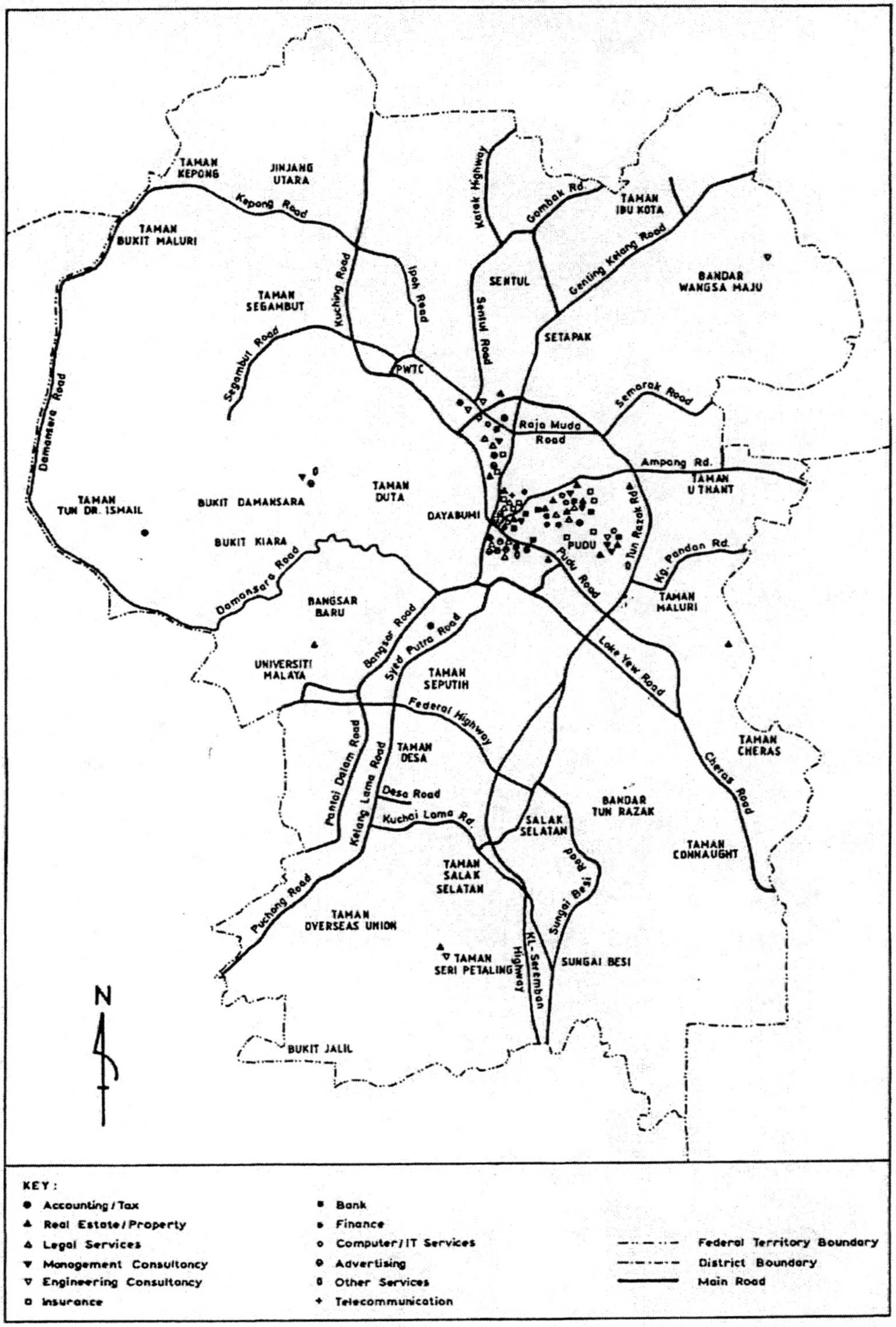

Table 5.1 Characteristics of Surveyed Producer Services Establishments

Ownership Structure:	
Single-site, local ownership	52.2%
Single-site, non-local ownership	4.3%
Single-site, non-local head office	3.3%
Multi-site, local ownership	29.3%
Multi-site, non-local ownership	6.5%
Multi-site, local and non-local ownership	4.4%
Legal Status:	
Individual proprietorship	13.0%
Partnership	23.9%
Public Limited Company	22.8%
Co-operative	1.1%
Public Corporation	4.3%
Private Limited Company	31.5%
Government Owned	1.1%
(Missing)	2.2%
Employment:	
Total number of employees contributed by surveyed establishments	25,760
Mean	283
Median	25
Mode	20
Malaysian	
Mean	282
Median	24
Mode	20
Non-Malaysian Citizen	
Mean	4
Median	2
Mode	1
Permanent Resident	
Mean	13
Median	2
Mode	2
Employment Trend in the Last 5 Years:	
Have Increased	70.4
Have Decreased	10.9
Have Remained Unchanged	18.4
Age Profile:	
Mean	17 years
Median	12 years
Mode	5 years

n = 92; Source: Authors' Survey

The 92 surveyed establishments contributed about 25,760 jobs in the Kuala Lumpur's economy as at end of March 1997. However, with respect to the size of establishment (number of employees), data indicate that there is wide variation. From Table 1, the median for the surveyed establishments is 25 employees and the mode is 20. A standard deviation of 1386 reflects substantial variation between establishments. So far as the number of Malaysian employees is concerned, the mean is 282 employees, and the median is 24 employees. But there are more establishments with only 20 local employees. The engagement of non-Malaysian citizens is not very rampant as compared to the employment of permanent resident. However, occasionally 44.6 percent of the surveyed establishments have to engage outside experts (both foreigners and locals) for their expert opinions/advices on specific matters. Training and MIS/IT are also normally provided by outside experts.

Out of the sample of 92 producer services establishments, 70.7 percent had increased employment in the five years prior to the survey and a further 18.4 percent had experienced no aggregate change in employment (Table 5.1). From the data, it could be concluded that most of the employment growth was additional in nature. However, it has to be noted that this survey was carried out before the financial and share market turmoil of July 1997. In-depth interviews, however, were undertaken when the country was experiencing difficulties.

5.3. Aggregate Performance of the Surveyed Establishments

The situation before the turmoil was quite clear. In so far as the clerical and related workers is concerned, 54.3 percent of establishments reported that they had to increase workers in this category between 1993 and 1997, while 30.4 percent reported that they had to maintain the number of clerical workers. Only 9.8 percent had to decrease workers in this category. 53.3 percent of establishments have engaged more professionals while 30.4 had to maintain their workers, and only 4.3 percent had to trim the number of professionals in their establishments. Evidently, while a little over 50.0 percent of establishments had to employ more clerical and related workers, a small majority (27 percent) acted on the contrary. Presumably, this had to do with increased usage of technology in particular computerization of certain work tasks in these establishments (Table 5.2).

5.4. Mobility and Locational Characteristics of Producer Services Establishments

In order to consider the contribution of producer services establishments to urban economic development in Kuala Lumpur, one important aspect to be looked at is the space-time dynamics of the producer services sector. The locational distribution of these activities within an urban area such as Kuala Lumpur has implications for employment, property-value and other related infrastructure development. For example, these activities were the major tenants of the massive office developments of the 1980s in central cities and selected suburbs of major North American cities, and they continued to be important considerations in local development and infrastructure planning (Harrington, Jr. and Campbell, Jr. 1997). In the context of American cities, certain services especially legal, advertising, and accounting services, have remained more centralized within the Central Business District (CBD) of large cities than the mix of clients they serve (O'Huallachain and Reid, 1991) gaining benefit from agglomeration of similar firms and employees. Arguably, this particular locational pattern is reflective of market structures allowing the high fees that enabled their use of expensive and prestigious office space (Harrington, Jr., and Campbell, Jr. 1997). How mobile are Kuala Lumpur's producer services establishments and what factors led them to select a specific location within the metropolitan area?

In terms of the length of time that the surveyed producer services establishments have been operating from Kuala Lumpur. A sizable majority (29.3 percent) of the surveyed establishments have been operating from Kuala Lumpur between 1981 and 1990. 26.1 percent of establishments were established since 1991. The mean and median numbers of years of operation were 17 and 12 years respectively, and the mode is 5 years.

No less than 41.3 percent of the surveyed establishments have, prior to operation at present site operated at different locations within Kuala Lumpur. 40.0 percent have before this operated within the city's boundary, and this reflects quite a high intra-metropolitan movement. The most common reasons cited for moving out of previous location were the need for more space because of expanding business activities (24.0 percent), the physical condition of buildings (6.5 percent), and the insufficient visibility of former location (6.5 percent). In fact, movers comprized largely of locally owned establishments. For single-site operations, the move to another location implied that they have to cease operation at the old site, whereas for multi-site operations the move would be seen as one that is aimed at capturing the Kuala Lumpur market segment. 26.1 percent of respondents reported that they have changed their operation site at least once since their establishment, and another 9.8 reported at least two movements in the past. The level of mobility among the surveyed establishments in Kuala Lumpur seems somewhat lower. Apparently, professional services establishments such as advertising, legal services, accounting, real estate and insurance services displayed a somewhat high degree of mobility. However, among this group of services, there is a high degree of locational stability; where a move has occurred, the origin and destination have tended to be within the Kuala Lumpur metropolitan area. Only very few establishments operating in Kuala Lumpur were previously located in other areas in the Klang Valley (1 establishment) or other major towns (1 establishment). 16.3 percent of establishments were contemplating moving their operations again at the time of survey. Evidently, the leading factor for this move was a desire to be located in visible or prestigious buildings/locations such as Phileo Avenue, MNI Twins Tower and other buildings/locations in the vicinity of the city's 'Golden Triangle'. Others cited client accessibility and/or low rental plus more space for out-of-Kuala Lumpur locations such as Petaling Jaya.

Table 5.2 Recruitment by Category of Workers between 1993 through 1997

Category of Workers	*(% Responses)*		
	Increased	*Decreased*	*Unchanged*
Professional	53.3	4.3	30.4
Non-Professional	21.7	1.1	19.6
Technical	34.8	4.3	16.3
Clerical and Related Workers	54.3	9.8	27.2
Marketing/Sales	30.4	3.3	19.6
General Workers	17.4	4.3	22.8
Supervisory	27.2	2.2	23.9

Source: Authors' Survey

5.5. SUMMARY

The characteristics of the sampled producer services establishments were as follows: the typical establishment was small, and a majority was independent, single-site and locally owned. However, their contribution to Kuala Lumpur's economy is nevertheless significant as their establishments have shown growth and expansion tendencies. As a result, the growth employment in the producer services appears to be associated with growth in the average size of establishments. The sampled establishments include a mix of activities of differing ages, with a large proportion being relatively new operations (sampled establishments had a median age of twelve years). This is not unexpected given the national trends in, and recent importance of, producer services sector.

Chapter 6

TRADE AND EXPORT OF PRODUCER SERVICES

6.1. INTRODUCTION

In the survey, respondent establishments were asked about their sales in order to establish the geography of their service trades and exports. This line of inquiry should enable us to answer a very important question of whether producer services contribute appreciably to the export earnings of Kuala Lumpur. Ultimately, we should be able to conclude whether producer services establishments in metropolitan Kuala Lumpur serve a very highly localized market or not. Relating ownership structure of producer services establishments in Kuala Lumpur with the geography of service linkages would enable us to infer the types of producer services establishments that need to be promoted in Kuala Lumpur in order to spur further urban economic development.

It has been argued in the context of the industrialized countries, (see for example, Palmer et. al. 1990), given that the primary role of producer services establishments as providing major support for the headquarters of locally based corporations in coordinating their activities, establishments in this category of services are non-dominant and growth dependent. On the other hand, producer services establishments depend upon services generated by local businesses for their survival and rely primarily on the support of and demand for local resources (Goe, 1994). However, empirical evidences suggest that producer services establishments have the potential of being non-locally dependent as they could rely primarily on the supply of and demand for non-local resources through the development of non-local trade (Goe, 1994).

The survey method adopted in the research reported in this book made it possible to relate characteristics of individual service providing establishments with out-of-region sale. Based on the data collected, certain pattern could be established with regard to the peculiar organizational aspects of producer service exports. For instance, establishment size or corporate linkages would probably influence the propensity to sell service outside local area. In the context of this research, "local area" refers to the Kuala Lumpur metropolitan area. Intra regional area refers to other areas outside Kuala Lumpur but within the contiguous Klang Valley. A research question in this study - whether producer service activities can bring income into the local area - could be answered by estimating sales outside the Kuala Lumpur metropolitan area. It is worthwhile to investigate at the same time whether Ashton and Sternal's (1978) findings in the case of New England that very small service firms were locally oriented while large firms were more likely to export out of the region holds true in the case of Kuala Lumpur. In contrast with the above, Beyers and Alvine (1985) and Michalak and Fairbairn (1988) found no relationship between firm's size and extra-regional export propensity among firms in the extended metropolitan Seattle area and metropolitan Edmonton, respectively.

In the research reported here, respondents have been asked to report whether or not they have extra-regional sales or sources of particular services, and while this could be reported in terms of RM (Malaysian Ringgit) worth of extra-regional sales, most respondents preferred to report in terms of proportion of total volume of sales. This, nonetheless, should enable us to identify the producer services sectors/establishments, which are most likely to obtain revenues from clients outside Kuala Lumpur area.

6.2. Trade Patterns Among Producer Services Establishments

In order to enable us to determine whether establishments depend upon local or non-local purchasers of services for their survival, questions were included to probe this aspect. In addition, information on the geographic scale of non-local trade was also requested from surveyed establishments. Indicators of the geographic locations of each establishment's sales were used to measure the geographic scale of non-local trade. Respondents were asked to estimate the proportion of their sales to various geographic locations. Responses to these queries were then used to determine whether the surveyed establishments engaged in local (Kuala Lumpur metropolitan area) or intra-regional (contiguous Klang Valley), inter-regional (other areas in Malaysia) and international markets.

The percentage of a surveyed establishment's sales to local and non-local markets was used to determine whether an establishment was locally dependent or non-locally dependent. Establishments with more than 50.0 percent of their sales in non-local market were classified as non-locally dependent while those with more than 50.0 percent of their sales in local market were classified as locally dependent since they primarily rely on local purchasers of producer services.

It was noted in earlier section that producer services establishments in the study were classified into various organizational set-ups and legal status based on their responses to related questions in the survey.

Arguably, non-local trade conducted by single-site establishments would involve transactions between independent establishments from other activities in different geographic locations. For non-local trade conducted by multi-site establishments with subsidiaries, branches or affiliates outside metropolitan Kuala Lumpur would involve internal co-ordination between headquarters and non-local establishments. It is this relationship that we should analyze in detail in order to assess how producer services establishments contribute to urban economic development.

Some notable patterns can be discerned from the data. Independently owned producer service establishments are more reliant on intra-regional sales and this would bring about upward demand linkages and downward supply linkages. In other words, independently owned producer service establishments are more likely to trade down the urban hierarchy than the non-independently owned establishments. There is a higher tendency for independently owned establishments to trade over shorter distances than non-independently owned establishments.

A broad and generalized picture arising from the data for geographic location of sales revealed that 39 establishments or 42.3 percent sold a substantial proportion of output to client firms outside metropolitan Kuala Lumpur but within the contiguous area of Klang Valley. Sales in Klang Valley ranged from a low of 10.0 percent of total volume of sales to a high of 80.0 percent. In comparing the figures for mean sales (25.6 percent) with that of median sales (20.0 percent) it can be concluded that there is a slight skewness in the distribution of sales to Klang Valley among the surveyed establishments. Even though respondents did not reveal information on revenues, it can be implied that these local markets are also important in terms of revenue.

Business services exhibited fairly high extra regional export propensities compared to professional services. But generally, the survey data highlighted the low level of direct international sales of producer services. Only 14 establishments or 15.2 percent reported overseas sales, especially to Singapore, Uzbekistan, Indonesia, Myanmar, Japan and Vietnam. However, 22 establishments or 24.0 percent saw the potentials for the export of producer services to destinations such as the Philippines, India, Papua New Guinea, Turkey, Hong Kong and London. However, except for London, others are still largely regional markets. Penetrations of export markets were made possible, so far, through promotional overseas trips but more often through the use of marketing consultants. Services of trading houses are also to some extent, an important marketing technique adopted. The use of MATRADE services is still very minimal indeed among producer services establishments as compared to the manufacturing sector.

A wider variation of export activities is displayed by the data collected. Exports ranged from a low of 1.0 percent of total volume of sales to a high of 70.0 percent. The substantial difference between the figures for mean export (17.2 percent) and median export (10.0 percent) further supports the anticipated and not so uniformed distribution of export activities among producer services establishments. What factors influence the propensity of some producer service establishments to export, i.e. to sell services not only out of Kuala Lumpur but also more importantly outside of Malaysia? Producer services sectors have never been perceived as export oriented, but lately their role in export market appears to have been stressed by the government. Even though the survey data set would not be able to illuminate the specifics of service exporters, detailed interviews will highlight some salient aspects of this group of producer services and the manner in which they operate. Factors that contribute to their export decisions or seek customers from outside their local area would become clearer.

Generally, however, trade among producer services establishments in Kuala Lumpur appears to be very localized in nature. This is contrary to the fact that Kuala Lumpur's economy is regionally if not, globally connected. This reality makes modelling of producer services exportability (as 'export base') very tenuous indeed. However, in terms of policy prescription, the increasing trend toward internationally joint ventureship of producer services would ultimately increase this 'export-base' possibility.

Structural characteristics, such as establishment size, ownership structure and organizational status of the establishments are possibly better indicators of export activity than location characteristics (see also Porterfield and Cox, 1991). Arguably, the fact that some establishments engaged marketing experts/specialists may increase the tendency to export needs examining in detail.

Previous studies (see Porterfield and Cox, 1991) have shown that high total annual sales are a significant predictor of export shares of establishments. However, in the study reported here it was not possible to determine this because sales were not reported in terms of monetary values.

6.3. Input Requirements Among Producer Services Establishments

In order to produce service outputs, establishments would normally require capital, labour, skill and technology. Arguably, the degree of intensity of requirement for all of the above varies greatly. Evidently, 54 establishments or 68.4 percent and 30 or 39.5 percent reported that services production is skill intensive and technology intensive respectively (Table 6.1). Only 27.6 percent of the establishments surveyed reported that their operations are capital intensive. Arguably, the rate of equipment investment in producerservices establishments surveyed is still low. However, the increasing trend towards skill and technology intensity would inevitably increase the rate of equipment investment. This is more so in view of the fact that we have seen a series of product innovations suited to producer services activities lately. In addition to the above influencing development, some categories of producer services - such as accounting, architecture, engineering and advertising - are particularly receptive towards new innovation and technology. Investment in technology, arguably, would lead to relative price reduction and enhanced performance (see for example, Perry, 1991).

Producer services establishments do buy other services and goods for the production of their services. Four main groups of other goods and service inputs considered as important/very important could be identified (see Tables 6.2-6.5). Computer and telecommunication equipment, and IT support services are often cited as required in the production of services. Arguably, if backward linkages including acquisition of local inputs and labour are strong, local impact is substantial. It must be noted however, that high export sales do not automatically create local economic activity unless some of the revenues from export sales are spent locally (Porterfield and Pulver, 1991).

The survey data illustrate broadly the regional imports situation of the surveyed establishments. 12 establishments reported goods and service inputs procurements from outside of Malaysia. Import ranges from a low of 2.7 percent of total value of import to a high of 50.0 percent. Interestingly, 44.6 percent of the establishments surveyed indicated that a significant proportion of goods and service inputs required are internally produced.

33.0 percent reported that their service inputs are acquired from other local firms, while 12.0 percent reported that inputs are sourced from outside service establishments but within the same organization. Others have various combinations of internally produced and externally sourced inputs requirements but none outweighs the other.

Table 6.1 The Degree of Intensity in Terms of Capital, Labour, Skill and Technology in the Supply of Services

	Degree of Intensity			
Items	*High*	*Medium*	*Low*	*Number of establishments*
Capital	27.6	47.4	25.0	76
Labour	35.1	45.5	19.5	77
Skill	68.4	30.4	1.3	79
Technology	39.5	52.6	7.9	76

Source: Authors' Survey

Table 6.2 Types of Other Goods and Service Inputs Required for Production of Services (Rated as Very Important and Important) - Group 1

Types of Goods/Services	% responses
Technology Goods/Services	32.0
Telecommunications/Media	12.0
Skills/Competency	4.0
Books	2.0
Client Entertainment/Satisfaction	8.0
Courier/Mail Service	2.0
Government Protection	2.0
Value Added Services	2.0
Computers & Related Equipment	6.0
Production Work	2.0
Design & Drawings	2.0
Authorities (Governing Bodies)	2.0
Facilities	2.0
External Services	2.0
Office Equipment	2.0
Training	2.0
Production of Signboards	2.0
New Products/Services	2.0
Communication Skill	2.0
IT Support	6.0
Response from Local/Federal Authority	2.0
Building Materials	2.0
Total	**100.0**

n = 50
Source: Authors' Survey

Table 6.3 Types of Other Goods and Service Inputs Required for Production of Services (Rated as Very Important and Important) - Group 2

Types of Goods/Services	% responses
Technology	6.9
Telecommunications/Media	10.3
Transportation	3.0
Skills/Competency	4.0
Power Supply	6.9
Books	3.4
Office Space/Working Environment	6.9
Client Entertainment/Satisfaction	3.4
Financial Regulations	3.4
Risk Management/Loss Control	3.4
Public Relation	3.4
Stationery	3.4
Best Practise Database	3.4
Systems Infrastructure	3.4
Computer Software	10.3
IT, Research & Development	6.9
Newspaper Advertising	3.4
Integrity & Honesty	3.4
Reinsurance	3.4
External Services	3.4
Data & Data Communications Line	3.4
Product & Marketing Information	3.4
Total	**100.0**

n = 29
Source: Authors' Survey

Table 6.4 Types of Other Goods and Service Inputs Required for Production of Services (Rated as Very Important and Important) - Group 3

Types of Goods/Services	% responses
Technology	23.1
Telecommunications System/Media	7.7
Transportation	7.7
Power Supply/Energy Services	7.7
Books	7.7
Marketing	7.7
Seminars	7.7
Stock Suppliers	7.7
Plan Printing	7.7
Legal Knowledge	7.7
Research Library	7.7
Total	**100.0**

n= 13; Source: Authors' Survey

Table 6.5 Types of Other Goods and Service Inputs Required for Production of Services (Rated as Very Important and Important) - Group 4

Types of Goods/Services	% responses
Telecommunications System/Media	25.5
Transportation	25.5
Office Space/Working Environment	25.5
Technical Support	25.5
Total	**100.0**

n = 4
Source: Authors' Survey

Among surveyed establishments acquiring goods and service inputs from outside the establishments, 8 establishments or 73.7 percent reported that their sources are located outside Kuala Lumpur/Klang Valley, and this ranges from a low of 10.0 percent of total volume of goods and service units purchased to a high of only 34.0 percent. In policy formulation one should not only be concerned with the export potentials of producer services. "Import substitution" is an equally important aspect to investigate. We should also look at ways to reduce leakages from the local economy. For example, Porterfield and Cox (1991) have reported that the larger the share of inputs purchased in-state, the lower the proportion of sales made out-of-state. However, while this suggests that in-state inputs purchases inhibit activity in export markets, these purchases keep the export money that is earned circulating within the state economy, enhancing the economic development process.

This analysis so far, offers some important insights into the nature of Kuala Lumpur's economy. Firstly, the Kuala Lumpur Metropolitan area, especially the City Centre represents a very important market for producer services establishments. Even if establishments are operating from the outside of the City Center, a major proportion of their clients are still located within the City Centre.

6.4. Client Profile of Producer Services Establishments

In order to reveal the primary source of demands for producer services, the surveyed establishments were asked to specify major and minor clients and the sectors to which they belong. This approach was adopted, as it is generally well known that establishments would be very reluctant to disclose revenue related data. Supply side surveys also provide a more rounded picture of the client base of establishments as no initial assumption have to be made regarding who the clients of these establishments will be (see for example, Juleff-Tranter, 1996).

From the survey, out of 31 establishments or 22.6 percent considered the agriculture sector as the major source of clients (i.e. more than 60 percent of their revenue comes from this sector). Similarly, for mining only 3 out of 17.27 or 11.1 percent establishments had construction sector as major clients. With respect to the manufacturing and service sectors the demand for producer services in both these sectors are roughly of equal importance. 37 out of 49 establishments or 75.5 percent had manufacturing based clients and 45 or 49.0 percent with service sector clients. Evidently many establishments had minor clients from the various economic sectors, except from the retailing/wholesaling sector (Table 6.6).

Table 6.6 Major (more than 60 percent of total business) and Minor Clients of Producer Services Establishments

Economic Sectors	Major	Minor	n=
Agriculture	22.6	77.4	31
Mining	11.1	88.9	27
Construction/Property Developers	83.3	16.7	6
Manufacturing	75.5	24.5	49
Retailing/Wholesaling	50.0	50.0	2
Services	78.9	21.1	57
Government	39.5	60.5	38

Source: Authors' Survey

The insignificant role of agriculture and in particular, the mining sector clients were apparently common to all types of establishments surveyed. Given the finding that a substantial proportion of establishments rely on the service sector based clients a substantial majority would also be buyers and users of services themselves. Earlier we have noted such tendency. It is to be expected that usage of services will vary between various types of establishments and in correlation with their ownership structure and organizational status. It is the smaller producer services establishments that show a tendency to externalise more of their service needs.

The survey data therefore seems to indicate that a relatively small proportion of producer services sales are to the agriculture, mining and construction sectors while manufacturing is an important source of demand for producer services. The service sector itself has also emerged as a significant source of demand for producer services, at least in numerical terms. It is not possible, based on the present data, whether this is also true in terms of revenues.

There is a tendency for locally owned establishments to be dependent on both manufacturing and service sectors as sources of revenue. In terms of legal status, these establishments are generally either private limited companies or companies established on the basis of partnership.

Evidently, very few establishments had trade only with one specific sector. Trade with either manufacturing or services sector appears to be associated with establishments, which are locally dependent. Trade with these sectors appears to have increased the probability of an establishment being locally dependent.

Externalization of producer services by both manufacturing and services sector appears to involve several factors related to the increasing complexity of the sectors concerned and external environment. Obviously, there have been general transformations in which goods and services are produced, in particular in relation to product innovation and differentiation. Services such as research and development, designing, advertising, and marketing aspects of the production of goods and services are vital to expansion and growth of these two sectors. The way goods and services are produced inevitably requires producer services inputs (process transformation). In their pursuit for greater efficiency, manufacturing establishments in particular, would introduce new tasks, functions and techniques. Technological changes apparently are occurring at a fast rate, and these had forced manufacturing establishments in Malaysia to seek specialized help externally. It takes time to develop internal capacities to deal with such changes. Smaller establishments would find internal provision very prohibiting.

For manufacturing and services firms, the national and global environments within which they must operate and make profits are becoming increasingly complex, in terms of finance, production and distribution. Even within Malaysia, functions relating to raising capital, foreign exchange and mounting or resisting take-overs and/or mergers is conditioned by government's regulations, which are constantly changing.

This expanding regulatory framework has increased the consumption of producer services. At the firm's level, the range of tasks related to the internal management and administration of the firm, and the co-ordination of intra-firm transactions, has expanded rapidly.

From the survey, only no less than 70.0 percent of establishments perceived that externalization of producer services is associated with non-cost factors related to the growing complexity of the business environment and government regulations. At the same time, no less than 50.0 percent of establishments survey cited the lack of technical expertise on the part of client establishments being another factor that has led to external sourcing. Surprisingly, 51.0 percent of establishments refuted the influence of pure cost-driven process of vertical disintegration on the part of clients that has led to a shift form in house to outside service provision.

6.5. Service Delivery

So far as local service delivery styles to local clients are concerned, face-to-face meeting is still very important and is widely adopted (Table 6.7). This is normally preceded or followed by facsimile transmissions or telephone calls. This second mode of service delivery is reasonably expected as a major style to deal with non-local clients. The use of electronic mail is still not widespread, even though it is acknowledged that this delivery style is getting popular, as it is cheap and fast. However, some respondents insisted that somewhere along the process of business dealings, face-to-face interaction is still necessary even though the cost of maintaining face-to-face contact between the producers, on the one hand, and their inputs and markets, on the other hand, is potentially the most expensive element of intermediate-demand service production (Coffey and Bailly, 1991). Evidently, this expense can be significantly reduced by spatial agglomeration. Evidence indicates that, unless the information transmitted is relatively standardized, new telecommunications technologies cannot be successfully substituted for face-to-face contact (Gottmann, 1977; Pred 1975; Tornqvist, 1970; cited from Coffey and Bailly, 1991). Coffey and Bailly (1991) argue that the conventionally held view that telecommunications technology will supplant face-to-face contact and thus produce a decentralization of producer services may be overly optimistic. On the contrary, it is possible that evolving telecommunications technologies will have the effect of increasing the concentration of these activities (see also Coffey and Polense, 1987a; 1987b).

Table 6.7 Service Delivery Styles

Delivery Styles	*Local Clients (%)*	*Non-Local Clients (%)*
Face-to-face	84.8	14.1
Fax/phone	82.6	44.6
Mail (Pos Malaysia)	64.1	34.8
Electronic Mail	28.3	25.0
Reports	5.4	2.2
Courier	4.3	2.2
Agents	1.1	0.0

n = 92 establishments
Note: multiple responses are possible
Source: Authors' Survey

6.6. Conclusion

Urban economic development policy, in particular in relation to larger urban areas, normally exhibits a service bias. Producer services as a sub-sector of services - could play an essential role in the development of urban regions. The survey findings appear to suggest that the development of producer services in Kuala Lumpur is mainly sustained through intra metropolitan trade linkages. Trade within the contiguous area of Klang Valley is also important for sustaining producer services establishments in Kuala Lumpur. The survey data lend support to the contention that producer services establishments in Kuala Lumpur are locally dependent since a substantial majority of establishments surveyed were found to engage predominantly in local trade and, by implications, depend largely on revenue derived from local markets. Only a small number of producer services establishments in Kuala Lumpur were engaged in export of services. The export capacity of this group of producer services is of policy significance. This study confirms that some producer services establishments are able to enter and compete in export markets. Arguably, this, in effect, creates a larger and varied pool of activities, which policy makers can draw from to stimulate the Kuala Lumpur's economy.

Although producer services establishments export only a small proportion of their service outputs beyond the Kuala Lumpur Metropolitan area and its immediate hinterland there are many indications that given the right approach and support they will be able to penetrate overseas markets, in particular emerging markets in South East Asia. Producer establishments appear more likely to be involved in export market if they employ consultants or specialists specifically for marketing objectives. But equally important is the fact that many took their own initiatives to promote their services overseas. Marketing assistance seems to be one pertinent area where government intention could become handy. These could be in the form of seminars and other public education strategies, focusing on marketing strategies, or it would be more relevant if technical assistance in terms of devising marketing strategies could be extended to producer services establishments which for some reasons are unable to have in-house marketing specialists.

Export levels outside the Kuala Lumpur Metropolitan area displayed wide variations. On average, even though the producer services establishments surveyed have lower out-of-Kuala Lumpur sales, they purchase a larger proportion of goods and service inputs within Kuala Lumpur. Arguably, even establishments that export little may contribute to urban economic growth if income spent on inputs remains within Kuala Lumpur. However, it is difficult to measure the contribution of producer services sector to metropolitan growth because of acute data problems. However, discussion in earlier chapters on the Kuala Lumpur's economy provides some indications of this contribution.

Producer services production appears to be technology and skill intensive, requiring presumably a larger technology and skill cost component. Backward linkages as indicated by the survey data, appear to be similarly confined to Kuala Lumpur economy.

Producer services establishments, which are active in export, seems to be those that are characterized by high total sales, and non-local ownership. However, it is still difficult to escape from the fact that the majority of service producers are locally oriented establishments.

The findings suggest that the main role of producer services in Kuala Lumpur is to support manufacturing and service sectors. These two sectors provided the most extensive source of trade of producer services establishments in the city. From the above, it appears that industrial development model is still relevant in the context of producer services growth in Kuala Lumpur. However, the findings provided significant evidence to support for the post-industrial model of development where the development of producer services is directly tied to and predominantly dependent upon the resources generated by the local service sector.

Chapter 7

SERVICE STRATEGY

7.1. INTRODUCTION

Strategies are important for the survival of any business organization including those that seek to provide producer services. In a sense, a strategy outlines the basic steps that management must take in order to achieve its objective or set of objectives. In general, they are broadly classified according to organizational levels as corporate-level strategy, business-level strategy and functional-level strategy. Corporate strategies address the issue of what type of business an organization is to be in and how resources are to be allocated among those businesses. Business strategies on the other hand, focus on the steps to be taken by the organization to compete against others in the same business. Finally, the functional strategies comprise the plans for achieving maximum resource utilization and efficiency in each economic and management function in support of corporate and business strategies.

Organizational goals are the other essential part of the whole management process and represent the desired end results, which the organization wishes to achieve through a series of strategies it sets forth for itself. Goals are important to the organization because they, among others: (1) help guide the direction and efforts of individuals and groups within the organization towards the attainment of the desired results, (2) affect how the organization's plans are made and its activities organized, (3) provide a strong foundation for motivating individuals and groups within the organization to perform at the highest levels of efficiency and effectiveness, and (4) form the necessary basis and standards of measurement for evaluation and control of its various activities.

Since goals and strategies form part and parcel of the whole management process, and therefore, are inter-linked with each other, the present section of the study wishes to delve into these two important aspects by looking at the relevant data gathered from the questionnaire survey.

7.2. Competitive Strategies

In order to survive a competitive environment, each organization must strive to achieve and maintain some sort of competitive advantage over others who are in the same line of business as them. Indeed this is the focus of business-level strategies of the establishment, which deal with the problem of how to compete with other establishments within a given business. Porter (1985) had identified five competitive forces facing an establishment in business, namely, the: (1) threat of new entrants, (2) bargaining power of suppliers, (3) bargaining power of buyers, (4) threat of substitute products, and (5) rivalry among existing competitors. Thus, to have a clear competitive advantage over other competitors, an establishment must be able to position itself firmly in the marketplace so as to gain an edge in successfully coping with these competitive forces.

Accordingly, Porter suggested three generic competitive strategies that an establishment can adopt in the pursuit of gaining sufficient competitive edge over its competitors, namely: (1) cost leadership strategies, (2) differentiation strategies, and (3) focus strategies. Cost leadership strategies focus on keeping costs as low as possible compared to those of competitors by way of maintaining efficient operations and exercising tight controls. The lower the cost the establishment can maintain, the lower is the price it can charge for its products. Thus, by keeping lower costs compared to its competitors means that it can compete with them on the basis of price. This strategy, not only enables the establishment to defend itself against price-war conditions by being able to maintain acceptable profits in markets dominated by such price competition, but also goes a long way toward ensuring customer loyalty by being able to consistently maintain the image as a provider of goods or services at lower prices than its competitors.

Differentiation strategies emphasize competing with all other establishments in the industry by way of offering goods or services that are perceived to be unique in the industry. The key to the success of this strategy lies in the ability of the company to make its customers see the uniqueness of the products it offers as compared to those of other establishments, and hence, will inadvertently be able to command the customers' willingness to pay extra for such differentiated products. Hence, unlike the cost-leadership strategies that are based on lower costs in order to maintain sizeable profit margins, this strategy enables the company to achieve similar profit goals by charging higher prices instead. The latter has been made possible by the customers' loyalty for its differentiated products.

The focus strategy differs from the other two strategies because, unlike them, it is directed toward serving the need of a limited customer group or segment only. This strategy thus helps a establishment build a competitive advantage or carve a market niche position by concentrating only on a selected portion of the market because of the belief that by doing so, the establishment will be able to utilize its efforts and available resources at its disposal more efficiently and effectively in providing products or services for its customers. Once the market segment is chosen, an establishment will pursue its strategic actions under this strategy by employing either a differentiation approach or a cost leadership approach or some combination of these two approaches. This is because, under the focus strategy, the establishment is able to either concentrate on containing costs (cost leadership approach), which are made possible by its now much limited operation or tailor its products or services to the special needs of its target group of customers (differentiation approach).

7.3. IS FOCUS THE KEY ELEMENT OF SERVICE STRATEGY?

In the context of establishments providing producer services in a developing country such as Malaysia (the focus of the present study), the more appropriate competitive strategy to be pursued by them should be the focus strategy. This is due to the highly competitive nature of the service industry and the severe constraints facing such establishments in the form of comparatively limited resources and relatively lower levels of professionalism, and as such, they are not expected to perform either as a cost leader or as successful providers of differentiated products in the face of unlimited competition from other establishments in the industry (for example see Sieh, 1992; Sieh et al., 1995). But however, if such establishments are able to segment their markets appropriately, and concentrate only on serving these markets, they may be able garner sufficient market niche by utilizing their limited resources more efficiently. The consequences of this strategy will be either lower cost approach or differentiation approach but applied within the confine of a specific segmented market.

On whether the establishments surveyed have indeed chosen the focus strategy as their preferred competitive strategy, Table 7.1 indicates majority support by the ratio of 3 to 1 (Support, 65.2 percent; Do not support, 20.7 percent). This finding has, to some extent, corroborated the intuitive contention made above that establishments in a developing country such as Malaysia would have to adopt a focus strategy in order to compete with others in this highly competitive producer service industry for reasons ranging from the relatively inadequate supply of resources, expertise, experience, and a host of other possibilities.

Table 7.1 Choosing Focus as the Competitive Strategy

Choice	% Response
Adopt focus strategy	65.2
Do not adopt focus strategy	20.7
Missing Response	14.1

n = 92

Source: Authors' Survey

To have a glimpse at the actual reasons why the establishments surveyed have adopted focus strategy, we tabulate the relevant responses in Table 7.2. It is seen from the table that the overwhelming reason for choosing the focus strategy is to gain some sort of competitive edge over other establishments in the competition. This includes, among others, the desire to secure sufficient market niche, stay ahead of competition, maintain the acquired market share, retain existing customers, and ensure the survival of the establishments' businesses. This category of reasons is general to all competitive strategies, and the fact that the majority of the establishments under study can only achieve them if the markets are segmented, i.e. focus strategy, it can only mean that these establishments are relatively less equipped and therefore less able to compete on equal footing against other establishments under unrestricted competition. The second most important category of reasons cited by establishments are the need to utilize the establishments' available specialized knowledge and expertise, and the desire by establishments to maintain good relations with both their customers and suppliers. The relevant establishments may have the required knowledge and expertise but yet they still need the segmented market in order to be able to usefully utilize them. This may well signify the establishments' lacking in physical and financial infrastructure to lend sufficient support. The need to maintain good relations with both the establishments' clients and suppliers is an obvious reason, irrespective of whether the focus strategy is adopted or not. However, since it is one of the important reasons cited for focus strategy, it may imply that the respective establishments were unable to fulfil it adequately under unrestricted competition, and have to resort to segmented market instead.

The need by establishments to differentiate their products and services speak of the stiff competition in the crowded market filled with establishments providing similar or close to similar products. As such, there is need for establishments to specialize in order to produce products or services that are uniquely different from those offered by other establishments. Accordingly the focus strategy is adopted. The last important reason given for choosing the focus strategy is the lack of options available for other strategies. This may be brought about by various constraints facing the establishments such as the lack of physical facilities, the specific and specialized range of establishments' set-ups and operations, established political connection and others. As such, the respective establishments have no choice but to adopt the focus strategy as dictated by the constraints facing them.

The next interesting question to resolve is how establishments in the study achieved 'focus'. Theoretically, once the market segment is chosen, the establishments in question may pursue the focus strategy through strategic actions which are either associated with the differentiation strategy or the cost leadership strategy or some combination of the two. Smaller establishments with limited resources will most often choose one of these two versions of the focus strategy, that is, a cost leadership version or a differentiation version, applied within a specific niche. Larger establishments with substantial resources and a wider product line on the other hand, will most likely employ various combinations of these two versions of focus strategy. In the study, focus strategy through the range of services offered by the establishments is taken as indicative of the cost leadership version of the focus strategy, while the focus strategic action of targeted customers represents the differentiation version of focus strategy. The rationales used to justify these choices are that, in the case of the former, the range of services offered would, in some sense, capture the effect of the decision on production costs and other related costs involved, while in the latter, the targeted customers indicates the choices made by establishments to differentiate their products in order to meet the needs of specific customer groups they have targeted. The finding of the study indicates that, out of 66 establishments which adopt focus strategy, 57.7 percent have achieved focus through targeted customers, 31.0 percent through the range of services offered, while the remaining 4 percent, have chosen both versions (Table 7.3). The implications of this result are twofold: (1) the establishments which employ the differentiation version of the focus strategy outnumber the establishments which adopt the cost leadership version by almost 2 to 1 ratio, and (2) the small number of establishments adopting both versions implies that most of the establishments which adopt the focus strategy are actually smaller establishments.

Table 7.2 Reasons for Choosing Focus Strategy

General Response	% Response	Actual Responses
Gain competitive edge	31.1	Gain market niche/stay ahead of competitors/maintain market shares/ retain existing customers and attract new customers/business survival/ maintain position of being the largest bank locally/gain competitive advantage/leverage on strength and customer base.
Specialized knowledge and expertise	18.8	Technical expertise/certain area and specialized area of knowledge/have better knowledge of location, pricing, demand and supply/know market better.
Maintain good relation with customers and suppliers	18.8	Customer satisfaction/good working relation with suppliers/gain customer confidence and loyalty/maintain close rapport with clients/gain public confidence and support.
Need to differentiate products and services	14.6	Markets flooded with similar agencies/differentiate from similar providers nationally and regionally/ specialize in principals/serve broader markets (if differentiate products and services).
Unavailability of other alternatives or options	10.4	Smaller office space/establishments only focus on shipping and manufacturing/no diversification possible/ operates as an offshore facility and hence products are limited/political connection.
Optimum utilization of resources	6.3	Maximise resources/ avoid spending resources thinly.

Source: Authors' Survey

Table 7.3 Choice of Strategic Actions of Focus Strategy

Strategic Actions	% Response
Through range of services	31.0
Through targeted customers	57.7
Both	4.2

n = 66
Source: Authors' Survey

Finally, we would like to re-examine again the establishments in the study that have not adopted the focus strategy as their competitive strategy. It can be seen in Table 7.1 that there is a rather substantial number of such establishments (20.7 percent or 19 out of 92 establishments), and it would be rather interesting to find out the reasons as to why these establishments have not employed the focus strategy. Unfortunately, we manage to get only 9 responses on this quest as can be seen in Table 7.4. Nonetheless, from those responses we can still get some idea as to the type of establishments that are involved, the kind of industry they are in, and the type of customers they are serving. It seems that the main reason why these establishments do not adopt focus strategy has a lot to do with the type of establishments they are and the scope of their operation. The relevant responses here seem to indicate that these establishments are large establishments which produce a wide range of products and services, have diverse operations over a relatively large market area, and strive to serve customers of multi-races. The second group of reasons pertain to the nature of industry the establishments are in. In this case, the relevant responses point to the specific Asian market region which they regard as being similar, and the competition within the industry as well as the changes in the deregulation policies, which would on the whole render it unwise to adopt focus strategy. Finally, the constraints imposed on establishments by customers also dictate their decisions not to focus. Here, the establishments cite reasons such as the customers' preferences for integrated common solution as well as the establishments' decision to produce only when requested by customers, and these provide some indications as to the kind of influences the customers have over the establishments.

Table 7.4 Reasons for Not Choosing Focus Strategy

Reasons	*Frequency of Response*
Diverse operations	1
Wide range of services offered	2
Asian region the same everywhere and therefore unwise to focus	1
Nature of the industry	1
Competition within financial industry and change in deregulation authority	1
Provide services whenever clients required	1
Customers look for integrated common solution	1
Produce multi-products and target multi-races	1

Source: Authors' Survey

7.4. Goals of Service Organization

As stated previously, goals are important to the organization because they, among others: (1) help guide the direction and efforts of individuals and groups within the organization towards the attainment of the desired results, (2) affect how the organization's plans are made and its activities organized, (3) provide a strong foundation for motivating individuals and groups within the organization to perform at the highest levels of efficiency and effectiveness, and (4) form the necessary basis and standards of measurement for evaluation and control of its various activities.

In the present study, establishments were asked to state the goals they consider important for the long-term success of their organizations. For this purpose, three goals were spelled out for establishments to choose, namely, profit maximization/cost reduction, risk minimization and administrative efficiency, beside other goals the establishments may consider important as well. The relevant responses from the establishments are given in Table 7.5. From the table, it is clear that most of the establishments do not pursue a single goal, but rather a series of such goals. Profit maximization/cost reduction has been identified as the obvious preferred choice of goal by most establishments, followed closely by the goal of administrative efficiency, and rather distantly, by the third most popular goal of risk minimization. The choice of profit maximization/cost reduction as the most widely chosen goal by establishments in the study is of no surprise as it is always the goal of any organization engaged in business to adopt this goal unless they are categorized as being non-profit business entity. In fact, this goal is relevant for all establishments, whether big or small, or whether it is a short run or a long run consideration when establishment is assessing its survival. As a matter of fact, it is even more puzzling to try and explain the reason why the remaining 12 percent of the establishments studied here have not adopted this as their organizations' goal.

Table 7.5 Goals of Service Organizations

Goals	n	Frequency	% Response
Profit maximization/cost reduction	92	81	88.0
Risk minimization	92	63	68.5
Administrative efficiency	92	78	84.8
Teamwork, coordination and communication.	92	2	2.2
Efficient day-to-day service	92	1	1.1
Staff (development) and training	92	1	1.1
Personal development in professionalism	92	1	1.1
Client satisfaction and excellent service	92	2	2.2
Become the best in industry	92	1	1.1
Have highly motivated employees	92	2	2.2
Idea generation and speed of delivery	92	1	1.1
Speedy and accurate service	92	1	1.1
Integrity (of management and business)	92	1	1.1
Low cost provider	92	1	1.1

Source: Authors' Survey

The somewhat surprising result here is the almost equal ranking of administrative efficiency and profit maximization/cost reduction as the organization's goals. The administrative efficiency is nevertheless a very important goal for any organization since each establishment has to trim its administrative wastage as much as possible by carrying the correct sizing exercises continuously in order to be able to redirect as much resources at its disposal towards the more productive sector. But compared to the profit maximization/cost reduction goal, which is considered more vital to the establishment's very own survival as a business organization, it is not expected to rank as high. Nonetheless, in view of the long term success consideration of the establishments as stressed in the questions asked, it would indeed add a very interesting dimension to be considered by the parties concerned. After all, increasing administrative efficiency would greatly contribute to the lowering of costs, and the latter would have a bearing on the profits earned by the establishments. And if we can add one point of speculation here, this result may imply that the local establishments studied may have considered themselves as being relatively inefficient administratively as compared to their foreign counterparts operating in this country, and thus there is an urgent need to focus attention on this goal much more than they would otherwise have done.

The risk minimization goal, chosen as the third most important goal in the study, is very much expected; in view of the more and more risky business environment the establishments are operating these days. To ensure their long-term survival and success, the establishments have to seriously assess the risks involved whenever they strike any business deal. Perhaps, out of sheer coincidence, since the study was partly done during the period of serious economic recession ever to face the country, the region, and the world at large, the risk factor facing the establishments may have ranked high in the minds of the establishments' representatives interviewed, and this may have contributed greatly to the choice made.

The other remaining goals chosen by establishments in the study rank much lower than the three goals discussed above. However, two interesting points to note on those goals are the important considerations the establishments seem to give to the human resource factor of the establishments and the clients they serve. The human resource related goals occurred three times in the list of the remaining goals in the form of teamwork, coordination and communication, highly motivated employees, and staff (development) and training, while the client related goal is in the form of client satisfaction and excellent service response. Each of these goals with the exception of staff (development) and training has 2 frequencies of responses as compared to only 1 response on each of the remaining goals in the referred list. This point goes to highlight the fact that the establishments are very much aware of the important role of the human resource factor in their organizations that they have to continuously undertake serious efforts to ensure their welfare by motivating them, encouraging teamwork, coordination and communication, and staff training and development. In addition, the establishments also appear to realize the need to keep their customers satisfied with the services they offer by ensuring excellent, speedy and accurate services at all time. It goes without saying that without customers' support for their products and services, the establishments' very survival will be on serious hold.

7.5. SUMMARY

This section started out by arguing that the establishments in developing countries would have to adopt focus strategy as their competitive strategy in competing with others in the same industry because of the highly competitive nature of the service industry and the severe constraints facing such establishments in the form of comparatively limited resources and relatively lower levels of professionalism. As such, they are not expected to perform either as a cost leader or as successful providers of differentiated products in the face of unlimited competition from other establishments in the industry. The result of the present study seems to lend support to such contention. It has been found that, out of 92 establishments surveyed, 65.2 percent have adopted focus strategy as their competitive strategy. On the reasons why these establishments have chosen to focus, the study reveals that: 31.3 percent have cited the gain in competitive advantage over others; 18.8 percent each mentioned the specialized knowledge and expertise the establishments have, and the need to maintain good relations with customers and suppliers; 14.6 percent cited the need to differentiate their products and services from others; 10.4 percent related to the unavailability of other alternative strategies; and 6.3 percent was due to the need to achieve optimum utilization of resources. Regarding the way focus was achieved, the finding of the study indicates that, out of 66 establishments which adopt focus strategy, 57.7 percent have achieved focus through targeted customers, 31.0 percent through the range of services offered, while the remaining 4 percent, have chosen both versions. This result seems to imply that the establishments which employ the differentiation version of the focus strategy (focus strategy through targeted customers) outnumber the establishments which adopt the cost leadership version (focus strategy through the range of services offered) by almost 2 to 1 ratio, and that most of the establishments which adopt the focus strategy are actually smaller establishments. On the reasons why some of the establishments surveyed did not adopt focus strategy, the responses highlight the scope of the establishments' operations that cover diverse area and offer wide range of products, the nature of the industry the establishments are in, and the constraints imposed on establishments by clients they serve.

Regarding the goals of the service establishments in the study, the results seem to indicate that they do not pursue a single goal, but rather a series of goals. Profit maximization/cost reduction has been identified as the obvious preferred choice of goal by most establishments, followed closely by the goal of administrative efficiency, and rather distantly, by the third most popular goal of risk minimization. The other remaining goals chosen by establishments in the study rank much lower than these three goals. However, it is worth noting that, the more important ones among these remaining goals seem to concern the human resource factor of the establishments and the clients they serve. This point goes to highlight the fact that the establishments are very much aware of the important role of human resource factor in their organizations that they have to continuously undertake serious efforts to ensure their welfare. In addition, the establishments also appear to realize the need to keep their customers satisfied with the services they offer by ensuring excellent, speedy and accurate services at all time. It goes without saying that without customers' support for their products and services, the establishments' very survival will be on serious hold.

Chapter 8

ESTABLISHMENTS' PERCEPTIONS

8.1. INTRODUCTION

Establishments' views regarding the kind of business environment they operate under and the prospects such environment entails for the establishments are of the utmost importance, not only to the respective establishments, but also to other establishments in similar business, as well as to the policy making authority, i.e., the government. Their perceptions regarding the market and its underlying forces, elements of competition, the kind of support given by the government, will all yield useful information for the establishments and their counterparts in the industry in assessing their level of competitiveness, prospects of success and potentials for future growth?

This section deals with the establishments' perceptions regarding: (1) the reasons for increasing demand for producer services in the market, (2) whether there are too many suppliers of the services the establishments are providing in the market, (3) whether the nature and basis of competition in supplying services has been fair, (4) whether there has been a high concentration of the services offered by the establishments in KL, (5) whether there are market entry conditions for the type of services the establishments are offering, (6) whether the government has been supportive with respect to the services the establishments are offering, (7) the chances of the establishments exporting their services outside Malaysia, and (8) appropriate actions deemed necessary to encourage local service organizations to export their services outside Malaysia.

8.2. REASONS FOR INCREASING DEMAND

The establishments were asked what, in their views, were the factors, which had contributed to the increasing demand for producer services in the market, out of the list of factors, given below:

1. Pure cost-driven process of vertical integration on the part of clients, leading to a shift from in-house to outside service provision.

2. Clients seeking services to reduce risks, cope with infrequent needs, and make it possible for the purchases of producer services to concentrate on skills core to the industry and market served by these establishments.
3. The lack of technical expertise on the part of clients.
4. Evolving relationships between producer service establishments and their clients in terms of service offered, and the relative importance of external purchase versus internal provision.
5. Non-cost factors related to the growing complexity of the business environment, government regulations, the need for third party information and other factors stimulating the demand for producer services not centrally linked to cost considerations.

The establishments' responses to these questions are recorded in Table 8.1. As can be seen from the table, the non-cost factors have been identified as the most important reason for the increasing demand for producer services with 59.8 percent responses received from the establishments surveyed. This is followed by the lack of technical expertise with 50 percent responses, clients seeking services 43.5 percent, and evolving relationship between establishments and clients 38 percent. The pure cost-driven process factor has recorded the lowest number of responses with only 23.9 percent. And again, since the percentages of the responses add up to more than 100 percent, it means that some establishments in the study have considered more than one reason in their responses.

Table 8.1 Reasons for Increasing Demand for Producer Services

Reason	n	Frequency	% Response
Pure cost-driven process	92	22	23.9
Clients seeking services	92	40	43.5
Lack of technical expertise	92	46	50.0
Evolving relationship between establishments and clients	92	35	38.0
Non-cost factors	92	55	59.8

Source: Authors' Survey

These results seem to imply that pure cost considerations are not the main driving forces, which make establishments seek the services from the service producing establishments. In this case, the choice of whether or not to fulfil the establishments' needs for services from the in-house sources or from outside the establishments, a decision which is based on cost factors, is not likely to be faced by most of these establishments. But instead, these establishments would most likely resort to seek services from outside the establishments, i.e., from other service producing establishments, due to circumstances, which are mostly beyond their control. Most of these circumstances are related to the growing complexity of the business environment, government regulation, the need for third party information and other non-cost factors stimulating the demand for producer services. In addition, there is an almost equally strong indication that the establishments are also forced to seek outside services due to the lack of technical expertise within the establishments. Some establishments have decided that it is more worthwhile to opt for outside services in order to reduce risks, cope with infrequent demands, and free as much of the establishments' resources and skills as possible for use in their core business of production. Finally, the long established good relationships between the establishments and their service-producing counterparts, which have developed over the years, have endeared the establishments to continue to prefer such services to the internally provided ones.

The present finding spells good news for the prospect of the producer service producing industry, at least from the perspectives of the establishments involved. The demand for producer services, as seen from the study, do not seem to arise from circumstances, which are under the control of the establishments. In situations where establishments can decide whether or not to seek services from outside sources, demand for such services from other establishments in the market, may or may not be forthcoming, depending on the costs involved. In other words, if the costs are unfavorable, the respective establishments may not seek outside services, and therefore, the demand for producer services in the market may not increase. However, in the present case where the demand for the producer services by establishments are mostly motivated by forces outside the control of the establishments such as, among others, by the increasing complexity of the business environment, government regulations, establishments' lack of technical expertise, established good relationships with service producing establishments, then the demand for such producer services by establishments will always exist. This kind of demand will certainly help boost the producer service producing industry.

8.3. Competition in the Service Market

Having determined in the above section that there exists potential demand for the producer services, and that the industry has a bright prospect of growing and expanding, the next interesting questions to pursue and resolve are whether the market for such services is competitive, where their concentration is, and how the government has responded to it. In determining the competitiveness of the market, the rough indicator used was the number of suppliers in the market. It is argued that, the larger is the number of suppliers present in the market, the more crowded the market becomes, and accordingly, more competitive. The relevant result, as shown in Table 8.2, has indicated that more establishments believe that the market for producer services is crowded since there are too many suppliers present. This result implies that the market for producer services, according to a greater majority of these establishments, is competitive.

Of related issue is the question of whether the competition in the producer service industry has been regarded as being "fair" by the establishments studied. The answer to this quest is given in Table 8.3. According to the table, a greater majority of the establishments believe that the competition in the producer service market is fair, with responses of 66.3 percent fair, 21.7 percent unfair, and 1.1 percent usually fair but sometimes unfair. However, since the number of establishments that consider the competition as being unfair is quite substantial, i.e. 21.7 percent, it is of interest to probe the issue further. After all, the issue of unfair competition is rather sensitive to a lot of people, especially those in authority, who in turn, may want to use such information to carry out some relevant remedial steps.

Table 8.4 lists the instances of unfair competition as claimed by some of the establishments in the study, grouped according to their possible links to the government sector, the establishments or both. It should be noted however, that the basis for such grouping is arbitrary, useful only as far as it facilitates the foregoing discussion. It is also felt to be of interest to note the similarity between the total number of instances of unfair competition here (Table 8.4) and the number of establishments which claimed that the competition was unfair (Table 8.3), an occurrence which is purely coincidental, even though there may be some implied significance attached to it. Starting with the government related instances of unfair competition of Table 8.4, it is seen that the complaints chiefly involve the specific rules and regulation, and the government policies in general, which may directly or indirectly hinder the fair play of competition, or give rise to some elements of bias in policy implementation, unfair system of tenders, restricted advertising, and highly regulated markets. While these statements may sound very general and lack the needed specifics for any possible reaction from the authority, they will serve as early warning signs that all is not perfectly sound and dandy with the system. Perhaps, those in authority should view these charges positively and act appropriately whenever possible.

Charges of unfair competition are also levelled against other establishments in the market, especially those that do not play by the rule. The rules and regulations, and the government policies may be sufficient and fair, but if there are establishments that do not follow the set rules, then this can also lead to unfair competition. In such cases, as implied here the responses, large establishments, by virtue of their large resources and influence, are able to do things which smaller establishments find hard to do, such as having the ability to secure the best of clienteles, undertake unethical rebating, charge unfairly for professional services, carry out excessive price cutting, charge undercutting fees unfairly, and unjustly exclude some services. In addition, some establishments may be competing unfairly by offering lower quality products and services, or by using unreal basis for competition such as advertising capability and the like, rather than real basis such as technical soundness and financial strength, while competing with others. On the other hand, both the establishments and the government may have their fair shares of contribution as far as the existence of unfair play field of competition is concerned, as well as the possible abuses in the usage of on line information. On final note, we would like to reiterate the point that, as far as the issue of unfair competition linked to the private sector is concerned, it is not sufficient for the authority to just introduce more and more policies and rules of the game in order to bring about fair competition, such policies must be the correct policies in the first place, and above all, enforceable ones. It is only then, can we ensure a fair play field for all.

8.4. Concentration of the Service Industry

The information on whether the producer service industry is concentrated in a particular area or spread out over several areas is a highly pertinent one. If it is concentrated over one particular area, and if the area in question also lies within or close to the neighbourhood of the industrial areas and townships which site the establishments in need of services, then the implication from it is that there may not be need for highly sophisticated telecommunication infrastructures to enable such establishments to have ample access to the required services provided. On the other hand, if the producer service industry were spread out over several areas and away from the areas where the establishments needing the services are sited, then the industry would need a well-developed telecommunication infrastructure to enable the services to be utilized effectively. On examining the related responses given in Table 8.5, it is seen that a high 75 percent of the establishments surveyed believe that the producer service industry is concentrated mainly in the Kuala Lumpur area. While this finding is not at all that surprising, in view of the position of Kuala Lumpur and its vicinity as the hub of growth and development for a long time, the fact that other industrial centres and townships are, of late, mushrooming in other parts of the country as well, there is a growing need for parallel development in relevant infrastructures to man this increasingly complex dispensation of services effectively.

Table 8.2: Are There Too Many Suppliers of Producer Services?

Response	Percentage
Yes	65.2
No	28.3
Missing responses	6.5

n = 92
Source: Authors' Survey

Table 8.3: Is the Competition in the Producer Service Industry Fair?

Response	Frequency	Percentage
Fair	61	66.3
Unfair	20	21.7
Usually fair but sometimes unfair	1	1.1
Missing response	10	10.9

n = 92
Source: Authors' Survey

Table 8.4 Instances of Unfair Competition

Instance	Frequency of Response
Due to Government	
Certain rules and regulations	2
Government policy	2
Bias	1
Tenders	1
Unable to advertise professional services	1
Highly regulated but allege non-compliance in markets	1
Due to Establishments	
Get the best clientele	1
Low quality products and services	1
Unethical rebating by other insurance brokers	1
Professional charges too extreme	2
Too much price cutting	1
Not based on technical soundness and financial factors	1
Undercutting fees for very small and very large organizations	1
MNCs exclude local advertising agencies	1
Due to Establishments/Government	
Unfair play field	2
On line information	1

Source: Authors' Survey

8.5. Market Entry Conditions

Of some relation to the issue of competition discussed previously is the issue of market entry conditions, imposed on new establishments entering the service market. While the imposition of such conditions may serve the purpose of ensuring that only the well-equipped establishments which have met certain specified entry requirements are allowed into the market, such conditions may, to some extent, hinder the smooth running of the competitive process of the market. Some new establishments, due to limited resources and experience, may be put to serious disadvantage if they have to stretch the already thin resources early in the game. Others may be put out of the market altogether if stringent entry requirements were imposed on them, and they cannot meet all of such requirements. All said it is obvious that the imposition of the market entry conditions will have certain influence on the functioning of the competitive process of the market. On this matter, our study has revealed that there are almost as many establishments which claimed that there are market entry conditions imposed as there are those which claimed otherwise, with a slight edge for the former (Table 8.6). This is a rather perplexing result indeed as the establishments in the study appear almost equally divided over the issue of whether or not there are market entry conditions in the producer service market, a position which leaves us with little or no lead for any kind of conclusion. At the most, the result seems to point to the fact that there is no uniformity amongst the service producing establishments on the issue of market entry requirements, such that, some establishments face the market entry conditions while others do not, depending on the kind and nature of the service industry they are in.

Since the majority of the establishments in the study have indicated the presence of market entry conditions, it is of considerable interest to take a closer look at some of these conditions. In Table 8.7, we list the instances of market entry conditions as given by these establishments. It is worthwhile to note here the near similarity between the total number of instances of market entry conditions given here in the table (40 responses; Table 8.7) and the number of establishments which claimed that such conditions exist in the producer service market (44 establishments; Table 8.6), an occurrence which is purely coincidental, even though there may be some implied significance attached to it. Going through the given list of conditions in Table 8.7, it is seen that the main responses given by establishments are related to the issues of licenses, appropriate qualifications for their staffs, government regulations, quota, the need to register and the approvals from relevant authority. Regarding the issue of licenses, which is the main condition cited, the establishments may have felt that there are simply too many licenses that need to be obtained, too many levels of authority involved, and that the process may have been much too complicated, time-consuming and cumbersome. This is followed by the requirement for the right qualifications for the staff the establishments hire, a condition that is very essential in this highly professional and competitive service industry, but one that the establishments may find hard to meet. The various forms and levels of government regulation, including the imposition of quotas in some types of services, the requirement for registration with relevant agencies, and the need for approval from appropriate authorities, are cited significantly, and may all be regarded less favorably by new establishments entering the service market, if those regulations appear excessive or too restrictive. The other remaining market entry conditions, though much less frequently cited, will be mentioned as well. They relate to the issues of getting the necessary recognition from relevant professional bodies, the government policies governing foreign ownership and minimum paid up capital requirements for establishments, and the need to show sufficiency in technical expertise and technology support. Lastly, there is this condition of free market entry and exit being cited, one that can be interpreted as referring to that necessary requirement which allows the possibility for entering and exiting the market by all establishments in the first place.

Table 8.5: Is the Producer Service Industry Highly Concentrated in Kuala Lumpur?

Response	Percentage
Yes	75.0
No	19.6
Missing responses	5.4

n = 92
Source: Authors' Survey

Table 8.6: Are There Market Entry Conditions for the Services Provided?

Response	Frequency	Percentage
Yes	44	47.8
No	38	41.3
Missing responses	10	10.9

n = 92
Source: Authors' Survey

Table 8.7: Some of the Market Entry Conditions Claimed by Establishments*

Entry Conditions	Frequency of Response
Quota on some operating establishments	3
Obtain required licenses	17
Register with relevant agencies	2
Approval from appropriate authorities	2
Government regulations	4
Appropriate qualifications	7
Recognition from professional institutions	1
Technical expertise and technology support	1
Minimum paid up capital requirement	1
Foreign ownership	1
Free market entry/exit is flexible	1

Original responses are rearranged by combining similar, close to similar, or related ones.
Source: Authors' Survey

8.6. GOVERNMENT'S ATTITUDE TOWARDS THE PRODUCER SERVICE INDUSTRY

The government's role in the market of any mixed economic system is essential. While not necessarily getting it directly involved in the running of the market, it can play the crucial role of guiding, motivating, and encouraging the markets in the direction it desires. The government, through its various policies, can have considerable influence in promoting the market's competitiveness or spur the growth of various industries in it. In particular reference to the producer service industry of the present study, the government is expected to have impact on the service market in terms of the influence it has on the: (1) competitiveness of the market, (2) fairness of competition, (3) growth of the industry, and (4) export promotion of services.

In promoting the competitiveness in the producer service market, the government can help by appropriately employing its policies in ways that will encourage as many players, i.e., producers of services, as possible to enter the market by removing as much impediments to its entry. As far as encouraging fairness of competition in the market is concerned, the government can lead the way by taking the necessary initiatives to remove those rules and regulations, and even policies, which seem to favor some establishments over others in the industry. Finally, in order to influence the growth and expansion of the service industry and promote the exporting of services outside the country, the government can adopt appropriate policies for the purpose in the same manner.

Examining the result of the study with regards to the establishments' views on the government's attitude towards the producer service industry, it is revealed in Table 8.8 that the establishments surveyed are mostly positive in their views, with 57.6 percent of the establishments feel that the government has been supportive of the industry, 13.0 percent are of the opinion that the government is protective, and 21.7 percent believe that the government has been uninvolved. Since in this section of the study, at least 70 percent of the establishments have considered the government as having favorable attitudes towards the industry, being supportive in 57.6 percent of the cases and protective in the remaining, and also, since in the earlier section of the study, it has been shown that the market for producer services was regarded competitive by most establishments with the demand for such services expected to remain strong, it is therefore expected that the industry is all set for rapid growth and expansion.

It is also worthwhile to try to suggest a hint at the possible explanation to account for the views of the 21.7 percent of the establishments that regard the government's attitude as being uninvolved. In view of the rather big majority of the establishments which see the government as being favorable in its attitude towards the industry, it is not easy to accept the claim that for the majority of the remaining establishments, the government has not shown any hint of positive support whatsoever towards such establishments. It is therefore quite plausible to suggest as an explanation, that the establishments in question are probably of the self-reliant types, which are not in particular need of specific government's supports. As a result, such establishments are not expected to make serious efforts to find out what the government's stand on issues involving the industry are or what kind of facilities it offers, and as such, these establishments remain largely ignorant of the government's position and concern.

Table 8.8: The Government's Attitudes Towards the Services Provided

Response	Percentage out of Total
Supportive	57.6
Protective	13.0
Uninvolved	21.7
Supportive and uninvolved in different ways	1.1
Missing responses	6.5

n = 92

Source: Authors' Survey

8.7. Export Potentials of the Producer Service Industry

The implied government's support for the producer service industry as highlighted in the previous section, should also be taken as indicating some sort of support for the efforts to export the services outside the country. This is because, such efforts would add additional demand for the locally produced producer services, which in the end, will contribute to further growth of the industry. This will be much in line with the government's stand on the matter, which indicates support for the industry on the whole, as earlier argued. However, it is interesting to find out the views of the establishments themselves regarding the possibility of their exporting the services they produce for the foreign markets. The result of such quest is given in Table 8.9. The responses given reveal that 59.8 percent of the establishments have ranked their chances of exporting the services as being good or better, with 17.4 percent giving the ranking of "very good". This result has to be interpreted very carefully since it may easily give rise to inaccurate impression if the interpretation is done out of its proper context.

Considering that the producer service industry is the more highly advanced, sophisticated, very highly professional and competitive kind of industry within the range of industries of any country, such show of confidence to export the services abroad, where the competition is expected to be much stiffer, is certainly surprising and, perhaps, better than anticipated of the local establishments such as those coming from a developing country like Malaysia. Even though, it has to be quickly pointed out that, there is a wide range of services offered within the industry, and that some types of services may be far more advanced and sophisticated than others, and that there is high possibility that these more advanced types of service may easily penetrate the foreign markets. Nonetheless, for most local producer-service-producing establishments, the export potential scenario is expected to be less rosy than indicated by the present result, unless the focus of the export destinations also cover the less developed and developing countries as well. Thus, the present finding, when taken within the context of these latter export market destinations, would appear more reasonable and within expectation.

To continue with the interpretation of the results in Table 8.9, and bearing in mind that the export market destinations for the locally produced services, as argued previously, may also involve the less developed and developing regions of the world, and perhaps, with some extended to the developed world, the results as given, appear quite promising for the growth of the export sector of the service industry. Here, 59.8 percent of the establishments feel that they have good or better chances of penetrating, and hence, competing in the foreign markets. That is indeed a good sign of confidence, a first condition in the long process towards realizing any dream. What is needed is further encouragement and support from many quarters, especially the government, before such dreams can be turned into some reality. However, there still remains a lot to be done with regards to the group of establishments that rated their chances of exporting their services outside the country as poor. This group, which accounts for 33.7 percent of the establishments surveyed, need to be given all the help and encouragement they need, firstly, to boost their confidence, and this to be followed by efforts to improve their competence, productivity, and last but not least, their level of competitiveness.

Table 8.9: Chances of Exporting Services Outside Malaysia

Response	**Percentage out of Total**
Very good	17.4
Good	42.4
Poor	33.7
Missing responses	6.5

n = 92

Source: Authors' Survey

In view of the implied good prospects for growth and expansion of the producer service industry, and its close dependence on the export sector of the industry, where the latter adds and complements the domestic demand for the locally produced services, boosts production and spurs further growth of the industry, the next section will discuss the views of the establishments regarding the various steps that need to be taken to encourage and expand the export sector of the industry. To achieve that, the establishments were asked to state whether the following actions were deemed appropriate as measures needed to encourage the local service organizations export their services to the foreign markets.

1. Initial stimulus on the part of the government to export marketing is required. Such marketing of services may be less costly relative to manufacturers' own international marketing efforts.
2. Financial assistance to establishments at or near an export threshold.
3. The trade – service resident in overseas embassies, should provide ongoing support.

4. Collaboration between the public and private sectors in service export development.
5. Government should assist service establishment in finding immediate market opportunities for service export.
6. Facilitate profitable joint venture arrangements with overseas service establishments to mitigate costs, as well as to enhance local market intelligence.
7. Export of producer services should be made an integral part of Malaysia's economic development strategy.

The establishments' responses to the above questions are recorded in Table 8.10. On examining the results, it is found that measures chosen by establishments to encourage the export of locally produced services, according to preference, can be grouped into 3 categories. The most preferred category of measures chosen by establishments consists of the need for the establishment of collaborations between the public and private sectors in service export development, facilitation of profitable joint venture arrangements with overseas service establishments, and inclusion of export of producer services as an integral part of Malaysia's economic development strategy, each with 63, 63, and 62 percent of responses respectively. The next preferred category includes the need to provide assistance by the government to the service establishments in finding immediate market opportunities for service export, and the need for the trade-services resident in overseas embassies to provide ongoing support, each with 53.3 and 51.1 percent of responses respectively. The initiative on the part of the government to provide the initial stimulus in exporting marketing, and the provision of financial assistance to the establishments at or near an export threshold, each with 47.8 and 42.4 percent of the responses respectively, have become a not too distant third place preferred category of measures chosen.

Table 8.10: Measures to Encourage the Export of Services to Foreign Markets

Measures	n	Frequency	% Response
Government's initial stimulus	92	39	42.4
Financial assistance	92	39	42.4
Ongoing support from overseas trade service	92	47	51.1
Collaboration between the public and private	92	58	63.0
Government assist service establishment	92	49	53.3
Facilitate profitable joint venture arrangements	92	58	63.0
Export of producer service an integral part of government policy	92	57	62.0

Source: Authors' Survey

On closer scrutiny, it can be seen that the given percentages representing the various measures chosen by establishments do not vary that widely since the range is only between 42.4 percent and 63.0 percent, and this can be taken to imply that those measures are roughly of equal importance. Putting the same point differently, it is argued here that, as far as the views of the establishments are concerned, we cannot dismiss any of these measures as being unimportant. We can stretch the discussion further by claiming that the results here also give some indication with respect to the establishments' preferences for long-term and permanent measures over short-term and temporary measures, and that the financial reasons are of lesser importance as influences in these choices. In these regards, we will argue that, the measures included in the most preferred category, i.e., collaboration between the public and private sectors, facilitation of profitable joint venture arrangements with overseas service establishments, and inclusion of export of producer services in Malaysia's economic development strategy, are all long-term and permanent measures, which are there to stay and to be pursued for a long period of time. On the other hand, the second most preferred category of measures consisting of the government assistance in finding immediate market opportunities and the ongoing support by trade services resident in overseas embassies, can be taken as short-term and temporary measures, which are expected to be dropped or become irrelevant, once the export sector in services is fully established and becomes self-reliant. Finally, the lesser important category of measures consisting of the government's initial stimulus to export marketing and financial assistance to related establishments, are clearly financial-linked measures, which, as can be seen, were regarded as being relatively less important by establishments.

8.8. Case Studies

The questionnaire survey findings reported in previous chapters provide some information regarding various aspects of producer services establishments in Kuala Lumpur. To investigate in some depth the role and potentials of producer services in the urban economy it is necessary to examine selected establishments in detail. Two case studies of establishments (accountancy and advertising services) which are no doubt supplying services to other firms or organizations and not individuals (see section 4.1) are reported here, in addition to one from architecture services to highlight further various aspects of producer services operation in Kuala Lumpur. A case study of IT firm is also included to highlight the perceptions of emerging producer service activity in Kuala Lumpur. Each case studies will consider in detail the profile of the establishments, their involvement or non-involvement in export of services and their perceptions and assessments of government support and assistance. The architect firm was chosen for its aggressive approach and practical recommendations with respect to exporting of architectural services abroad. The case of the IT firm reflects the city's ability or rather inability to accommodate new and emerging service activity.

8.9. Case Study 1 (Accountancy Firm)

8.9.1. Introduction

The firm presented in this case study is one of the big six accounting firms and has been operating in Malaysia since 1928. It is a multi-site local firm, established through partnership arrangement with a multinational firm. Currently, it employs about 1,000 people at its head office in Kuala Lumpur. Its branches nationwide are located in Ipoh, Penang, Johor Bahru, Malacca, Sandakan, Kuching, Labuan, Kota Kinabalu, Tawau and Kuantan. Its organizational practices are quite similar to that of a franchise whereby its operators are locals and the branches are independent sites. However, resources are shared widely between local and international branches. The costs of providing the resources or expertise are borne by the branches concerned. Arguably, such organizational set-up is deemed appropriate to legally protect professionals working for the firm's "subsidiaries". In the likely event of cessation of operation of a subsidiary, the employees are not professionally liable (cancellation of license to practice etc.) plus the parent firm would not be affected. Thus, the organizational set-up enables the firm to have global presence with minimum risk.

8.9.2. Core Activities

Initially, the firm was an accounting service provider. Eventually, the firm diversified into several other services namely taxation, corporate finance, corporate recovery (strategy services) and management consultancy, which are divided into two sub-units: Executive Search & Selection and Enabling Technology (IT Services). The types of services offered vary according to the economic climate and depending also on the time of the year. Interestingly, the firm noted that due to the nature of its business, it has a competitive advantage during both economic slowdown and upswing.

During the economic crisis of 1997/98, two types of services were experiencing substantial increase in demands, and these were

1. Corporate recovery i.e. liquidation, firm restructuring, corporate strategy services. Companies need to be responsive to the local and international markets changes and adapt to these changing circumstances quickly. Companies also need to find ways to sustain their operation by venturing into other sectors that could still provide positive returns on the basis of existing resources.
2. Some companies were faced with limited options to deal with consequences of economic slowdown; most however opted for the easy way out, staff retrenchment. CS1 offered an "outplacement" package under its Executive Search and Selection Division. Companies wanting to retrench their staff saw the need to update or refresh their executives, especially their senior executives, as to how to write CVs, handling questions during interviews, how to create

presentation and so forth. All these were taken with a view to enable these executives present positive images of themselves to prospective employers.

On the other hand, the training services, which were in great demand before the economic crisis were experiencing steady decline. Since the economic slowdown, companies chose to tighten their belt and consequently there were very few staff training programmes.

Interestingly, during the economic downturn there were noticeable increase in the demand for comparable services provided by smaller accounting firms and they charged a substantially reduced fees. If during boom time CS1 considered the "big six" accounting firms as its major competitors, during difficult period competition came in the form of small, independent local firms. Realizing this, CS1 changed its strategy in its effort to keep its accounts by giving discounts or negotiating directly with client firms for service provided. To CS1 giving discount appeared to be a much better option than getting paid through instalments during a time of credit uncertainty whereby payment may not come through after all.

8.9.3. Operating Issues

CS1 has indicated in the questionnaire returned during late 1997 that it was going to merge with one of the six big accounting firms. However, the deal was called off after evaluating the costs and benefits to both companies and their clients. With six accounting firms to choose from the business community will have better choices compared to only four companies, if the merger has been successful. Furthermore, the decision was necessary to avoid a near-monopoly situation in the existing market. Another reason for the decision not to follow through the merger exercise, and this was considered of great importance given the nature of the accounting business, was the need to maintain a high degree of confidentiality of serviced clients. Merged companies would be faced with the likely possibilities of servicing clients' competitors. From the point of view of clients of both firms, they would rather terminate their accounts with these firms then faced with the problems noted above.

With respect to the question of the future of small accounting firms, CS1 felt that mergers among smaller firms would be inevitable in order for them to stay competitive in the open markets. A much larger organization with several employees would be able to send some of these employees as representatives to keep the company up-to-date on changes in procedures and regulations, which affects business operations. Small firms would not be able to do the same for it would cause backlogs in existing job assignments. Therefore, for CS1 size was important for continuous success in accounting services.

In terms of information technology awareness and usage, the firm's employees were mostly PC-literate. The firm was highly integrated with its branches nationwide and affiliates worldwide through electronic mails. IT experts in the firm's Enabling

Technology unit provided professional services in setting up new accounting systems for clients' companies.

8.9.4. Problems in Importing or Exporting Services

CS1 reported that accounting firms would be faced with several problems when attempting to export their services to foreign markets. The major obstacles being the following:

1. Problem of local certification/licensing requirement to operate in different countries or to qualify for practice in host country for a firm must be a member of the host country Professional Institutions (this is sometimes hard to obtain due to stringent guidelines).
2. The foreign firms would be required to employ locals provide services to their clients.
3. Closed-door policy on professionals attempting to operate in the host country.
4. Joint ventures or partnerships with locals in host country could possibly be terminated once the local partners have gained professional recognition and have enough experiences to go solo.

On the other hand, the firm indicated that the kind of business it conducted did not require heavy dependency on foreign expertise. CS1 hired foreign expertise during the initial set-up of the firm in Malaysia and the Asia-Pacific region. The reasons are:

1. Limited knowledge on local regulations and practices of accounting and taxation.
2. The firm preferred to send its local staff for training or attachment (secondment) overseas to gain expertise due to attractive government's tax-breaks for training costs.

But, in certain circumstances it had to engage foreign experts; and the government's aspiration to have an electronic government in place is good example to cite. Malaysia, admittedly, does not have the expertise to set up electronic government on its own. It is vital for Malaysia to learn from other countries, which have a fully operational system in place, for example the US and the UK. In the longer term employing experts from these countries would have certain benefits and advantages for Malaysia; these experts had vast experienced in trying to implement electronic government system. Otherwise, CS1 was committed in hiring and training locals especially fresh graduates with Accounting and IT majors, as part of its strategy to offer diversified services from its multi-skilled workforce. CS1 also expressed preferences for employees to "grow with the firm" rather than hiring highly experienced candidates who would not have the kind of loyalty the firm required.

Besides being a supplier of services, CS1 was also a buyer of other producer services in the open market; it will hire other local professionals such as lawyers, and investment bankers to work collaboratively with them on client's projects.

8.9.5. Impact and Influences of Government Regulations

CS1 acknowledged the fact that the frequent changes in Malaysian government's regulations on accounting and taxation practices were inevitable due to the dynamic nature of the industry. The firm nonetheless realized that it had to keep abreast with the constantly changing government regulations to stay competitive. Towards this end, it was quite usual for CS1 to engage ex-senior government officials (for example retired custom officers) to update it on changes in government's regulations and their implications for the accounting and related services.

Evidently, non-cost factors related to the growing complexity of the business environment, government regulations, the need for third party information and other factors stimulating the development for producer services not centrally linked to cost considerations have resulted in noticeable increase in the demand for CS1 services. CS1 expressed dissatisfaction and reservation over the present government's regulation that has affected its ability to market openly its range of services. The regulation prohibited advertisement of professional services except allowances for name, address, contact persons, telephone and fax number in business directories. The firm argued that this regulation restricts its marketing effort to advertise aggressively its wide range of services, which undeniably was also its competitive advantage. Other countries are flexible on this aspect. Furthermore, the information in business directories did not have detailed description of the types of services offered by them. Arguably, the range of services offered varied according to the economic circumstances of a particular country.

CS1 proposed a partial relaxation of regulation pertaining to the way accounting services were being offered and that the market for these services in Malaysia be opened up in stages. At each milestone, the government should assess the supply and demand situation for accounting and related services in the country. This would enable the government to monitor the progress of the industry and subsequently exercise better control and supervision. In addition, CS1 recommended an examination of aspects relating to practising licenses for professionals in host countries. There is always a possibility of formulating a reciprocal arrangement between Malaysia and another country with respect to allowing professionals in Malaysia to practise in that particular country and vice versa. Besides helping to bring up services in Malaysia to international standard, this would also directly promote exporting of professional services. However, there is a possibility of Malaysia experiencing an outflow of professionals if the participating country offers higher remuneration packages.

8.10. CASE STUDY 2 (ADVERTISING FIRM)

8.10.1. Introduction

CS2 has been operating in Kuala Lumpur for over six decades. Initially, it was registered and operating under different name. However, after being taken over by a US-based firm, CS2 became one of the companies in the global network and operated using the name of the acquiring firm. Its core business was advertising but in recent years the firm has diversified into other areas of marketing communications e.g. public relations, direct marketing, interactive marketing and event managing and promotions. CS2 is now a foreign-based firm with 51 percent Malaysian interest. CS2 list of clients is very impressive, comprising of twenty well-established MNCs and major Malaysian corporations. The firm currently employs a group of about 100 people at its Malaysian sole office-site. Apart from its foreign CEO, other employees are Malaysians.

CS2 is relatively small in comparison with other major advertising firms but in this industry size is determined by billings (the amount paid for media) and revenue. Currently, CS2 is one of the top 10 firms in terms of billing amount in the advertising industry. However, the firm felt that size was immaterial for it preferred to stay small and maintain a manageable list of clients. For CS2, by maintaining a short list of clients, it could provide consistently high quality service, which was important for business. The firm was focused on offering the most varied advertising services in the country and worldwide through vigorous investment in its most important asset- its employees. The firm invested heavily in training programmes for their employees so as to realize its vision of offering the most varied services through their multi-skilled and multi-talented workforce. Subsequently all these would transform CS2 as a reputable job-training agency in the country.

Interestingly, the firm introduced flexible working hour in conjunction with telecommuting for the benefit of its creative workforce. The firm realized that creative ideas do not emerge during fixed working hours. This proved to be beneficial to both parties. The firm gets committed and responsible workers delivering consistently high quality work piece within the specified timeframe. This policy is complemented by the available infrastructure that facilitates telecommunicating among the staff, enhancing further employees' comfort while working at home, in the office or elsewhere.

8.10.2. Locational Characteristics

Initially, the firm chose to operate from Kuala Lumpur because most of its clients' headquarters were located within the Klang Valley. Therefore, it make sense at that time to also start an operation in Kuala Lumpur and at the same time make their presence felt in a prosperous region.

As the telecommunication infrastructure improved, the firm felt that there was no need to be located in the centre of the City of Kuala Lumpur as physical presence was not vital. It could continue to communicate on a regular basis with its customers electronically. CS2 finally decided to relocate to building, which was accessible and conveniently situated for the benefit of both employees and clients. Due to the nature of the organization, which relied on teamwork environment, maintaining high interaction among employees was viewed as critical. Ways and means to promote this environment must be found. Thus, the firm preferred one whole floor to relocate all its employees. Safety was also important since many of its employees had to work well into the night; and security measures could easily be enforced in smaller buildings. Finally, the building must have the required infostructure for electronic communication.

The above criteria were reflective of the firm's continuing concern over its employee's welfare and comfort at the workplace. Obviously, it was also a positive approach in dealing with creative people by trying to provide an ideal working environment that would help promote the generation of creative concepts and ideas.

8.10.3. Advantage/Disadvantage of Being a Foreign-Based Firm

The firm strongly felt that foreign-based firms have many distinctive competitive advantages over their local counterparts. These advantages helped them forged forward aggressively and gained recognition and market share in the local market, as well as in the region.

The main area that local firms could not match was in tapping the networked resources of international firms. The firm acknowledged the potentials of the advertising industry in Malaysia but it would be a while before it could be at par with similar service-producing firms in advanced countries in terms of the quality of the advertisements produced. The firm cited Bangkok as an excellent case of local firms being able to produce world-class quality advertisements for the simple reason that local advertising firms have the opportunity to work with foreign experts. For Malaysian advertising firms to be known internationally, Malaysian firms need to win a lot of local and international awards for their advertisements. Local firms must also benchmark the industry's best production in the world, instead of measuring up to meet local standards only. However, this is impossible to achieve if there were limited cross-border learning and participation. Admittedly, local Malaysian firms should tap into the rich network of resources to upgrade the local advertising industry; by either creating a link to professional bodies of the advertising industries or becoming affiliates or associates firms of international advertising companies. Affiliation or association could be done through memorandum of understanding (MoU) without sacrificing financial or equity structure of the firms concerned. In return, the international agencies that were not represented in Malaysia but needed someone in Malaysia who could work with them as and when opportunities arises could benefit from the arrangement since opportunities are irregular to warrant setting up an office or a joint partnership.

Apart from the above, CS2 also conducted in-house training by bringing its own experts from another region and admittedly by doing this the firm manage to save on fees paid if it were to hire industry experts from another firm from another region. The cost of hiring the international trainer was shared among several markets where the international firms were present. Indirectly, the network of companies promotes economy of scale. In comparison, local companies had to pay 100 percent of the fees if they hired an international trainer. Currently, the practice has become very expensive and uneconomical due to weaker regional currency.

Being part of a much larger international agency has some drawbacks for CS2 in particular with respect to staff's skills development. For instance, it is not unusual for work in a much larger agency to be more departmentalized and specialized. In a much smaller agency, however, employees had the advantage of being cross-trained and consequently learnt many more skill over a period of time.

8.10.4. Firm's Responses to Government Regulations

CS2 was not infavor with the "protectionist policy" of the Malaysian government in so far as the advertising industry is concerned. In its view protectionist policy was appropriate initially when the industry was struggling but now it has matured and very competitive the policy has to be scrapped. Now the industry welcome the gradual easing of deregulation measures so that it has the flexibility to operate effectively with resources available. Sadly, according to CS2, tight regulations and closed-door policy of the Malaysian government have become serious hindrances to the industry. Its ability to compete and rise to global standard has been seriously hampered. Taking as an example, CS2 pointed out that the recent advertisement on the *Commonwealth Games 1998* by Filem Negara (National Filem Corporation) was clearly a piece of work based on outdated technique and style and was a minus for the advertising industry in this country. The Filem Negara's *Commonwealth Games 1998* would certainly reflect badly on the Malaysian advertising industry as a whole for it continued to use technologies of the 60s and 70s even when the state-of-the-art media and technology are available in the market and have been used by others in Malaysia.

The firm seriously believed that by opening up the local advertising industry, local advertising agencies would be able to learn substantially from the more advanced markets. The effect would be a continuous upgrading of the quality of Malaysian advertising. The local agencies would then have a basis of comparison, which inevitably, would impose higher standards in the production of advertisements in the country. Local agencies could then benchmark with "the best in the world" instead of the "best in Malaysia".

Another issue that CS2 was not satisfied with relate to government's ruling on the number of expatriates that agencies could hire at any one time. The firm argued that the condition for the hiring of expatriates should be determined by the size of a firm; current regulation, however, calls for a fixed number of expatriates regardless of size of the firm. According to CS2, there were occasions where agencies need to hire expatriates exceeding the number allowable because some talents or expertise were just not available locally. In addition, expertise was limited to a few areas, or worst, one area only.

The firm further expressed its dissatisfaction over the regulation that did not allow a firm to hire foreign directors unless there was special permission from FINAS, the national film body. The firm argued that the best work in the world was and is being done by a handful of directors. If locals were going to learn from these directors, they have got to see the directors in action and work alongside the directors. Therefore, the firm felt that if this restriction was relaxed, it would have been easier for the industry to bring in people known to have produced the best work and initiate technology and skills transfer to the locals.

Lastly, the firm felt that the government together with the industry should start exploring the many opportunities in terms of realizing the export potentials of this service. The firm proposed that the government promotes advertising services overseas in the same manner it has promoted the telecommunication services abroad. The firm, however, made the assumption that besides lacking government support in promoting the Malaysian advertising industry, the local advertising services have not been able to export their services because local players have not been able to establish themselves in the international advertising market as producer of high quality, state-of-the-art advertisements.

Interestingly, CS2 was of the opinion that Malaysia has natural advantages in the field of advertising services. For instance, the country is blessed with many "nature scenes" e.g. sunny day, rainy day, desert-like areas, wetlands, tropical climate/plant, mountains and so forth. Malaysia has yet to exploit these natural scenic surroundings in its advertisements.

8.10.5. Firm's Response to the Economic Crisis

Based on CS2 responses, the most important determinant of success in the advertising services, besides its creative people, is how well the firm manages its credit collections. The profit margin in the industry was very small and therefore the firm had to insist on prompt payment from its clients for work completed. Many establishments, having being paid extremely late by clients, had to forgo major portion of their profit to paying penalty for late payment to their creditors. It is usual for advertising agencies to put upfront payment to media agencies for work advertised on behalf of clients.

The problem of late payment was noted as part and parcel of operating advertising agencies. The recent economic and financial turmoil have greatly affected clients' ability to settle their accounts promptly. Consequently advertising has a tough time collecting payments and the already small profit margin among advertising agencies were being further eroded. CS2 has been very proactive in dealing with this problem by taking several measures to discourage delayed payment for services rendered. First, defaulters will be penalized at a rate of 1 percent on payment made later than the allowable 30-day payment period. Second, clients who are prompt or made early payment will be given a discount of 20 percent on billing amount. Having introduced these "stick and carrots" measures CS2 discovered that local companies continued to display a longer payment cycle than international firms. International firms were more likely to pay promptly and save on early payment discount. CS2 would next consider introducing a ban on advertisement for two months for clients who failed to settle their account promptly.

CS2 also noticed that during period of economic expansion, clients were more aggressive and adventurous and would readily accept innovative advertising ideas and approaches put to them. They were able to see the effects of advertisements in the longer term and were very concerned with establishing or building brand names. During difficult times however, clients were more likely to take a conservative stance and requested minimal experimentation or exploration of otherwise innovative ideas or concepts. Generally clients were preoccupied with sale volumes and short-term benefits or solutions. Clients were more likely to request for discounts on billable amount for services.

8.11. Case Study 3 (Architecture Firm)

8.11.1. Introduction

CS3 has a long track of excellent record in architectural practices in Malaysia and overseas. The firm has designed many unique buildings for an MNC from the US operating in the Klang Valley and a recently completed tower for a major political organization, which gained recognition from other architects in Penang Island and abroad. The firm specialized in designing bio-climatic buildings it claimed that there are few firms offering the type of services they are engaged in.

In the difficult period of 1997, while many other establishments offering designing services were experiencing serious operational problems CS3 continued to operate for it has development projects overseas. These projects were started even before the onset of economic downturn. CS3 had to trim its staffing strength in order to be leaner and to cope with an expected drop of almost 67 percent in business volume. The economic downturn wiped out two years of accumulated profit. One of the major factors affecting its profit level was the amount of salaries paid to staffs, which incidentally was based on boom time rate.

8.11..2. Firm's Marketing and Positioning Strategy

In contrast to other local architect firms, CS3 has been aggressively promoting itself overseas through various means so as to position itself in the international market. The firm reflected that it had taken 10 years to do just this internationally. However, locally it is already a well-known and established architect firm. Generally, the firm marketed itself through publications such as books or shorter articles on its achievements in magazines, participated in annual trade exhibitions worldwide, and direct marketing to potential clients. For instance, in 1997 the firm participated in a trade exhibition in New York, USA, and, in 1998 it attended the trade exhibition in Berlin, Germany. The marketing materials distributed to clients or potential clients include:

1. Firm's brochures
2. Monographs which published assignments undertaken by the firm

3. Catalogues for trade exhibitions
4. Postcards

The firm admitted that monographs were usually sponsored because they were expensive to produce. According to the firm, it had to first establish good relationships with publishers and editors of magazines before they would agree to publish a monograph for the firm. In addition, a third party, who would explore and comment on work undertaken by the firm, usually wrote a monograph. Thus, the writer had to be of some credibility in order for the monograph to be highly regarded by readers.

As for catalogues and brochures, the firm had to make sure that the materials done are of world class since the brochures and catalogues would reflect the firm's image. In addition, the firm also sent postcards to keep in touch with its clients and these usually portray buildings that it had completed. It is also a way to tell the clients that the firm is still operating. CS3 has been adopting these marketing and promotional strategies since the eighties and now it is gradually reaping the benefits. According to CS3, foreign architect firms have pursued almost similar marketing strategy.

CS3 targeted Taiwan and the Middle East as potential markets for its services. However, CS3 admitted that the Taiwan market was a hard one to penetrate because of Taiwanese pro-American mind-set. Nevertheless, the firm is still determined to go in and promote its expertise. In so far as the Middle Eastern region is concerned, the firm specifically targeted Dubai due to the encouraging local planning policy and the city's vision of becoming the 'Singapore of the Middle East', with its own notable high-rises, financial and retail centres.

It should be noted, however, that the firm has international presence in other countries primarily in Singapore, Adelaide, and Japan. In Singapore, it holds about 20 percent equity in a local firm, as this arrangement is necessary for it to bid for government contracts, and to penetrate the Singapore market. In Adelaide, CS3 is engaged primarily in building resorts. The firm went into the Australian market with a Malaysian client, only later to become its business partner in Australia. The firm also collaborated with Japanese architects for work in Japan. On a smaller scale, the firm was involved in a project in Italy. In the UK, the firm has been short listed for a project in Sheffield. Besides, practicing in these countries, the firm also actively participates in international architectural competitions in Taiwan, Singapore and Argentina as an alternative way of introducing its architectural services.

8.11.3. Potential Exportability of Architectural Services

Primarily because of the downturn in economic fortunes, Malaysian services firms are now starting to explore opportunities overseas. Going abroad has become a matter of necessity for these firms to deal with current problems. CS3 felt that local architect firms have to reflect on their acquired expertise during the boom time and the list will be a long one. Admittedly, local architect firms have accumulated valuable experiences during the period when the local economy was booming. Malaysian architects were already exposed to many aspects of the design and building services due to rapid development of office buildings, high-rises, highways, hotels, resorts, residential units (low-cost, medium-cost, bungalows lots, condominiums) and bridges following the period of economic boom. The extensive experience coupled with strategic marketing to potential target markets abroad could be a starting point for exportation of specialized architectural services. Besides specialized services, we could also export highly skilled labor to target markets. Positive impact on balance of payment of services would likely result from the fore mentioned activities. Evidently, architect firms should embark on strategies to publicise the types of specialized services available in Malaysia and simultaneously stimulating a demand for these services.

The firm cited some interesting examples that are exportable or unique and these are:

1. Malay style houses, resorts that is suitable for areas with similar climatic conditions. The rich texture and cool interior of the Malay house has been proven to be appropriate in Egypt.
2. Hong Kong developers are known to engage Malaysian architects for Master Plan designing in China. Evidently, Hong Kong architects are familiar with micro town planning but Malaysians are quite adept in generating Master Plan for larger areas, and more importantly developers need not pay hefty sum for Malaysian services.
3. Other expertises with export potentials are specialized services in building high-rise structures, long-span bridges, and highways.

8.11.4. Government's Role in Promoting Services – Firms' Perception and Recommendations

CS3 opined that the government did not play an active role in helping to promote Malaysian services. So far, the firm was able to promote its services due to extensive personal contacts it has over the years. CS3 regarded MATRADE as playing an important role in the promotion of manufactured goods but not with respect to services in particular producer services. The firm recommended several initiatives that the government could take towards helping to promote services. First, the government could help in compiling comprehensive market information in targeted countries with respect to future projects at the blueprint stage, local regulations and practices, local custom etc. Second, to proactively encourage trade mission to target markets so as to create awareness of services available from Malaysia. Third, to help identify companies and developers in target markets related to architectural practice with a view towards collaboration, partnerships and linkages.

Other recommendations for the government to help stimulate export of services, in the context of setting new venture overseas, include the following:

1. Trade exhibition with foreign architects

2. Government-owned companies, which had penetrated market overseas and made their presence felt, should help promote other Malaysian companies.
3. For government projects overseas, for instance the building of government offices and embassies, priority should be given to Malaysians. These projects when completed would become promotional features for Malaysian service providers, in particular architects.

On the basis of CS3 experiences when going abroad, the firm noted that good business relationship, and a demonstrated sense of awareness of the sensitivity of host country's architects towards foreign architects are extremely important. These two aspects if handled properly by foreign architects could help eliminate professional barriers and some of the hostility shown towards foreign architects.

8.12. Case Study 4 (Information Technology Firm)

8.12.1. Introduction

CS4 is a new Bumiputra (indigenous Malaysian) company with 42 employees. The company started out with a fairly small paid-up capital of RM 400,000. Later on, it formed a partnership with a state development agency to increase its paid-up capital. The company's main business activity is developing customized software for clients. This includes application development for electronic government systems, and network products i.e. network integration, electronic commerce etc.

8.12.2. Location Characteristics

Previously, CS4 operated in a building in the heart of Kuala Lumpur, in a premise rented from the Selangor State Economic Development Corporation. CS4 decision to move its operation from Kuala Lumpur to Universiti Putra Malaysia (UPM) Incubation Centre, Selangor was due mainly to high rental rates in the city centre. It felt that by re-locating to UPM, the company could utilize available resources from UPM. For example, UPM students could be a reliable source of knowledgeable workers and UPM lecturers could be engaged as IT consultants. In addition, UPM's close proximity to the Multi-Media Super Corridor (MSC) is an advantage to the company.

However, with economic downturn, city centre' rental rate is significantly cheaper in comparison to the one it is paying at the new location. For, even with economic downturn there was no reduction in rental rate at the Incubation Centre location. The company has raised this issue with the landlord, Malaysia Technology Development Corporation (MTDC), but to no avail. MTDC gave the reason that the rental rates at UPM were on a contractual basis, therefore is non-negotiable regardless of the predicament the firm was experiencing. To make matter worst, CS4 was also paying rental for unused spaces, which was to have accommodated projected expansion of business. The rental for the use of premises was more than RM 10,000 per month, or 20 percent of the company's fixed overhead cost.

8.12.3. Operational Problems and Constraints

CS4 were faced with financial limitation that has affected its growth prospect. It was unable to recruit "knowledge workers" to handle current projects or to carry out advanced developmental work on current products. Admittedly, IT workers are highly specialized and they normally command higher pay. Attracting them to CS4 would be very expensive.

Financial limitation means less ability to fund development cost for systems commissioned by clients. Normally, CS4 has to cover all the costs related to system development and client/customer would only pay CS4 if and when the systems were fully developed and operational. Occasionally, clients failed to settle payments due even after the system was ready and running with the excuse that the system did not meet their requirement and specifications. From the point of view of CS4, this situation has arisen because clients failed to furnish all information relating to their needs and expectation. Clients sometimes failed to define their business and did not specify clearly their requirements to system developer. Normally, system development would initially involve an in-depth discussion between clients and system developer to chart out clients' requirements and preferences. Defining customer's requirements accurately is critical as it determined the system design and development. Modification to a developed system is very expensive and would require much more man-hours. Clients' feedbacks and comments are required at every stages of the development of the system. CS4 would normally request clients to review system under construction properly so as to minimize modification due to changes in requirements. Non-payment on the part of clients for reasons, which arise from clients' own shortcomings, is one of the most frustrating part of the IT business. However, once IT market in Malaysia has matured, the problem would be minimized greatly.

Quite related to the problem of finance is the fact that quotation as per tender (to the government sector in particular) is normally below the actual costs of developing the system. The IT industry is highly volatile and unpredictable giving rise to substantial escalation in cost. Quite often, by the time the tender is processed and awarded, new technology and new prices are being released into the market. The firm then would be in a dilemma, as the tenderer now called for the latest system to be delivered. Supplier is obliged to comply and to provide the new technologies at the cost of the old technology per the original quotation sent to the government. In addition, the company also faced longer payment period from the government i.e. on average 60 days compared to the 30 days the firm has to pay the vendor. This situation has aggravated further the financial position of the firm.

CS4 perceived that the non-Bumiputra IT companies would have strong financial position due to backing and support from members of the so called "bamboo network".

The firm felt that financial support from the government through the local banks was a welcome move in order to help boost the IT industry. However, financing for IT companies is a very tricky affairs in the absence of clear guidelines from the banks on how loans are being awarded. CS4 felt that collaterals such as land, houses etc. are no longer valid when dealing with IT companies.

With respect to employment, at the time of interview CS4 had 42 workers, of which 17 were permanent staff and 25 part-timers or free lancers. Apart from that, the firm also engaged university students as part of their practical training programme. CS4 has the advantage of being able to employ knowledge workers from the pool of IT graduates from UPM and some final year IT students from other local universities. CS4 has targeted final year IT students with the hope that when they graduate they would continue working with the firm. Those that decide to stay on would normally demand higher pay for now they have already some experience in IT product development. Admittedly, employee's turnover in the IT industries is high due to high demand for experienced IT professionals in the sector.

When faced with the financial and recruitment problems, CS4 normally resort to the engagement of free lancers. With this group of workers, there is always the possibility of missed deadlines since they normally worked on other projects simultaneously. This group of workers require close monitoring of work progress. CS4 admitted that its ability to engage academic staff from UPM as consultants is an advantage. CS4 has been given the approval to engage these staff whenever the need for them arise. To date, it has succeeded in developing systems on a small projects basis with the involvement of UPM staff and students. However, in so far as the long-term scenario is concerned, CS4 felt that Malaysia lacked adequate supply of knowledge workers. The current supply of this particular group of people is sufficient to help the firm's on-going operations for a while but not enough to help it expands.

8.12.4. Export Potentials

At present, CS4 is focused on developing system for internal market only. The firm felt that exporting activities involved much higher risk but would explore this opportunity in the future. CS4 was very optimistic in its plan to export their products to regional markets, for instance Indonesia, Thailand and Brunei, probably in two years time. A main consideration would be efficient networking in the marketing of products.

At present, CS4 is involved in an electronic government project with a local telecommunication and IT giant, namely, SAPURA. This local company has developed Executive Decision Tool Software, which it hopes to be able to market successfully through SAPURA's parent company, which has excellent marketing and distribution channels. The software, once endorsed by the leading software manufacturer, would gain positive recognition and eventually market confidence. SAPURA has tried to market the software itself but was unsuccessful. One of the reasons given for this failure was the prejudice towards Malaysian IT products, as the IT industry in the country is still in the developing stage.

8.12.5. Firm's Perception on Government Roles

CS4 was confident that it could develop world-class applications if it has sufficient resources. The firm stressed that a good product needs a lot of research and development (R&D and this activity requires a substantial amount of financial outlay. Without it, R&D efforts would be severely constrained and subsequently product features would be affected. However, the irony being without a product, CS4 would not be able to apply for further financing to enhance its R&D activities on the said product. Financial limitation constrained CS4 efforts to further develop system applications.

The company felt that MTDC, as the developer of the MSC is not doing enough for the local industry. MTDC, in selecting firms eligible for grants, imposed very stringent rules and is very bureaucratic. One of the criteria set is that firms have to demonstrate uniqueness in the kind of service they are offering. CS4 argued that to survive, a company should not be too unique or highly specialized as demands would not be enough to sustain the company's operation. CS4 felt that uniqueness could only be developed later on as the company progress. It is also felt that the MTDC has become more like a real estate agent, selling land and properties at Cyberjaya or from its land bank.

8.12.6. Recommendations to the Government

CS4 strongly urged the government to play an active role in ironing out problems pertaining to the disbursement of loan to IT companies. CS4 commented that the government should bear in mind the nature of IT business and products. It is unlike other sectors of the economy that the government is used to dealing with. The government needs to guide the banking sectors on how to disburse the loans accordingly and what proper measures to be used in selecting deserving applications from IT companies.

CS4 felt that there is a strong needs to educate the general public on the usage of information technology. By doing so, it is hoped that the industry would expand through high demands for its services. Clients must be able to determine their system requirement and for this they have to be knowledgeable on various aspects of IT uses and environment. While customer's requirements no doubt would become more complex and sophisticated in the future but if these were clearly defined it would be technically challenging for IT firms

CS4 implored on the government to speed up the processing of tender applications and reduced the red tape. Technological changes in the IT industry are very rapid. Time lag between tender submission and tender approval would render the original tender submission useless for new technologies are being introduced in the market. The government's practise of approving tender and specifying that new technology is to be supplied put many IT firms at a disadvantage. The government needs to be aware of the conditions surrounding the IT company operations when calling for tender submissions.

8.13. Discussion and Conclusion

The first half of this chapter deals with the establishments' perceptions regarding various matters involving the producer service industry, namely, the demand for the services, issues of competition, concentration and market entry conditions, the government's attitudes towards the industry, and the export potentials of the services produced. The finding on the demand for producer services reveals that for most establishments in the study such demands are primarily caused by non-cost related factors that are mainly beyond the realms of the client-establishments' decision-making and control. As such, the demand for the services by the client-establishments will exist, irrespective of these establishments' positions, the latter, especially, with regard to costs. In that respect, the prospect for the growth and expansion of the producer service industry has become brighter.

With regard to competition, most establishments studied believe that the producer service industry is competitive, and that the competition in the market is fair. On the issue of concentration, a big majority of the establishments feel that the industry is mainly concentrated in the Kuala Lumpur area. However, there is no such clear-cut difference between the establishments that feel that there are market entry conditions in the producer service markets and those establishments that see otherwise, with 47.8 percent of the responses representing the former, and 41.3 representing the latter. As far as the government's stand towards the industry is concerned, at least 70 percent of the establishments have considered the government as having favorable attitudes towards the industry, being supportive in 57.6 percent of the cases and protective in the remaining.

The establishments have ranked their chances of exporting their services to the foreign markets rather positively, with 59.8 percent of them having ranked such chances as being good or better. While this is indeed a good sign of confidence on the part of the establishments involved, further encouragement and support from many quarters, especially the government, are needed before such dreams can be turned into some reality. However, there still remains a lot to be done with regards to the group of establishments that rated their chances of exporting their services outside the country as poor. This group, which accounts for 33.7 percent of the establishments surveyed, need to be given all the help and encouragement they need, in order to boost their confidence, improve competence, raise productivity, and last but not least, increase their level of competitiveness.

Finally, on the measures needed to encourage the establishments to export their services to the foreign markets, it was argued that the measures suggested are roughly of equal importance, since the percentages of the establishments' responses on these measures do not vary that widely, with the range lying only between 42.4 percent and 63.0 percent There is also further indication from the results, that establishments generally seem to prefer the long-term and permanent measures to boost exports, comprising measures of the collaboration between the public and private sectors, facilitation of profitable joint venture arrangements with overseas service establishments, and inclusion of export of producer services in Malaysia's economic development strategy, over such short-term and temporary measures of the government assistance in finding immediate market opportunities and the ongoing support by trade services resident in overseas embassies. Finally, the financial-linked measures, such as the government's initial stimulus to export marketing and financial assistance to related establishments, are regarded as being relatively less important by establishments.

In the second half of this chapter, three case studies of producer service establishments have been explored in greater depth. All the establishments examined are in different stages of export penetration. Very few have been exporting their services overseas prior to the crisis of 1997. The crisis in fact has triggered the need to explore potential markets overseas for some. Otherwise, with sufficient opportunities domestically, they do not see the urgent need to venture outside of Malaysia. The case studies reveal specific and general strategies pursued by establishments. Future and potential strategies that need to be adopted were also highlighted. The role of government agencies and other supporting institutions were identified.

Ideally, MATRADE, need to develop a general strategy to promote, facilitate and assist service (professional) firms to penetrate foreign markets (for example see Morshidi and Sharifah, 2000). In so doing, it is expected to provide market information on opportunities abroad, organizing specific promotional programs, conducting technical seminars in selected high-potential markets to highlight Malaysian technology and expertise. MATRADE has been appointed as the focal point for the projects funded by UNDP to increase the procurement of Malaysian services by UN agencies. MATRADE improves the knowledge of Malaysian exporters on various aspects of international marketing through organizing seminars and workshops. It publishes and distributes ***Malaysian Services for Export Directory*** with the aim of disseminating information on Malaysian services abroad. Sadly, while MATRADE is experienced in handling promotion for the manufacturing sector overseas, its involvement in promoting professional services is a very recent one. There are indications in the past for MATRADE to overlook the specific requirements of professional services establishments relating to export initiation.

On the part of Export-Import Bank of Malaysia Berhad (EXIM Bank) it is a well-known fact that Malaysian professional services firms are quite reluctant to export services because of the high risk involved. Inadequate financing on the part of these firms made such a venture not attractive. EXIM Bank's role is to promote the export of Malaysian goods and services through the provision of short to long-term credit to Malaysian exporters. One that is of relevant to professional services firms is the export of services facility. The purpose of this facility is to assist Malaysian services firms to export their professional services overseas. In so far as professional services firms are concerned, the financing scheme will also cover export marketing. It is acknowledged by EXIM Bank that as at the end of 1997 only one computer firm has been extended the export service facility. EXIM Bank acknowledges that extending this service to professional services establishments is fraught with problems and difficulties. Financing of service export is a new experience for EXIM Bank.

It is also worth noting that Malaysian government export promotion via MATRADE seems to be more concerned with helping firms rather than managers. There are obvious reasons for targeting managers and not firms. Arguably, programs such as trade exhibitions, trade missions and country-market seminars typically target potential exporters. The objectives of doing so are to increase market awareness and knowledge, initiating exports, and penetration of potential markets. But there is no clear distinction in governmental promotion strategies with respect to matching information, promotion, exports financing with firms at different levels of export involvement (pre-engagement, initial or advanced stages).

Available research into the marketing of professional service in the US have indicated quite strongly that professional services need to be considered separately from product and non-professional service marketing because traditional consumer models and concepts cannot be easily interpreted for professional services (Bloom, 1984; Lovelock, 1981; Gummesson, 1979; cf. Marr, *et. al.*, 1996).

Promotional activities are the major marketing activities for a professional service establishment, and except for some aspects of advertising, all areas of promotion are person intensive and often require the involvement of highly qualified professionals (Marr, *et .al*, 1996: 547).

It is quite obvious that a serious rethinking of export strategies is needed. The Seventh Malaysian Plan has embarked on a bold step to include export of services as an integral part of Malaysia's drive towards an industrialized nation status. However, this should not be seen by service providers as a 'stop-gap' measure to deal with contracting domestic demand for services. In order to promote export of professional services, service establishments themselves need to consider seriously the possibility of joint venture arrangements with overseas service establishments to mitigate prohibitive costs, as well as to enhance local market intelligence. MATRADE's role is still important. Over the years this agency will be able to accumulate experience in handling the promotion of Malaysian professional services overseas. MATRADE must assist professional service establishments in finding and identifying market opportunities. MATRADE is good at this. In order to be effective, trade-service residents in overseas embassies must supplement MATRADE's role. Financial assistance must be extended to service establishments at or near export thresholds. But, unlike manufacturing industries, professional services establishments have nothing tangible to prove to EXIM Bank of their worth and risk situation. Arguably, in order to deal with this difficulty professional services establishments need to assemble their portfolios in terms of completed projects overseas and a list of reputable referees. This must be complemented by a careful examination of EXIM Bank's guidelines on export service facility, which to this date has been too stringent. EXIM Bank's qualifying criteria in terms of the strength of the establishments (financially and expertise-wise) is in it very prohibitive.

Chapter 9

CONCLUSION AND POLICY IMPLICATIONS

9.1. INTRODUCTION

The primary objective of the research reported in this book has been to explore the role and contribution of producer services activities in the urban economy, specifically Kuala Lumpur through in-depth analysis of both primary and secondary data. In this concluding chapter the findings will be assessed in terms of their relevance to the role of producer services in the growth and development of urban economy in Malaysia. Of particular importance will be the policy implications of the research findings in the context of urban development and planning of Kuala Lumpur. The findings no doubt will be of some relevance to other globalizing cities of the more advanced developing countries in general. However, it has been clearly established that the service sector is heterogeneous in nature and the findings may only be relevant to urban economy experiencing rapid development in the producer services sector in particular rather than service sector in general. Nonetheless, in certain aspects the findings do have broader relevance and implications and these will be highlighted.

This research began with a synthesis of various strands of theories and explanation within the producer services literature. The role and contribution of producer services in urban growth and development have been determined through an exploration of related literature. In order to appreciate the growth of producer services in the context of an urban economy it has been necessary to explore and draw on a range of theoretical and empirical literature concerning externalization of producer services, trade in producer services, export of producer services, localization of producer services at the metropolitan level, and manufacturing-service linkage. The review of literature serves to highlight the growing importance of producer services in the urban economy, both in terms of employment and as a source of GDP. In particular the role of export of producer services has been emphasized.

The Kuala Lumpur producer services sector has been explored at various levels of details. Firstly, at the general level the role of the sector in the growth of the Malaysian economy and that of Kuala Lumpur have been established. Evidently, Kuala Lumpur tops the nation in terms of growth and development of this sector. Second, the specific contribution of certain sub-sectors to the economy of Kuala Lumpur have been established, at the same time declining service activities have also been highlighted. Questionnaire survey serves to probe further the role, and potentials of a broad spectrum of producer services establishments in the city, noting also constraints and problems that need policy intervention. Detailed and in-depth analysis of the contributions of two important and expanding activities have been made. Detailed interviews with selected representatives of some of the major service sectors have been conducted in order to comprehend and determine underlying factors influencing decisions making at the establishment level. These interviews were conducted at the time when Malaysia was experiencing financial and stock market turmoil and appropriately the interviews revolve around the questions of promoting the export of producer services and the scope for government's intervention and assistance.

The findings of empirical research presented in this book make an important contribution to our understanding of the role of producer services in urban spatial economies experiencing a shift from manufacturing to services (for example see O'Connor and Edington, 1998; Daniels, O'Connor and Hutton, 1991). In this concluding chapter the major findings of the study will be summarized and assessed in terms of their relevance to urban policy making. Subsequently, its contribution will be considered, and the questions that it raises highlighted. Some suggestions for future research directions will also be noted.

9.2. The Role and Contribution of Producer Services

This study has highlighted the importance of producer service activities in the growth and development of Kuala Lumpur. The producer services sector – operationalized in this study according to the Browning-Singelmann typology - experienced noticeable growth at least between late eighties and middle nineties. The largest source of new jobs occurred in business services such as advertising, and some professional services such as accountancy and engineering.

There is some evidence to support the view that the growth of producer services in Kuala Lumpur could be linked with the organization of capitalism at the global level in particular the 'international spread of manufacturing, corporate-related (producer) services, and the development of a system of international financial markets'. The concentration and growth of producer services in Kuala Lumpur could be viewed as partly being driven by the increased demand for producer services by multinational corporations as corporate ownership has become more concentrated in the Klang Valley and the geographic scope and complexity of their operations have expanded. Producer services growth is also attributed to government's regulations aimed at making Kuala Lumpur competitive in the national and global urban hierarchy as location for high-technology industries and advance producer services

Evidently, producer services in Kuala Lumpur assist locally based multinational corporations and other local business organizations in attaining dominant exchange positions in local and regional markets for their respective industries. The central business district of Kuala Lumpur accommodates a substantial number of producer services establishments creating a 'corporate complex' within the urban spatial economy. In general terms, a corporate complex is defined as a social network with the administrative unit of a firm providing a hub that is linked with a group of local business establishments from producer services. Producer services establishments primarily depend on local trade with the administrative units of hub firms. Notably, the linkages among producer services in the case of Kuala Lumpur require geographic proximity. The reason for this is increasing traffic congestion problems and locational and corporate building images consideration.

It appears that local producer services establishments have not played a significant role in the global market place for producer services. This explains the low level of exchange through non-local trade with administrative units of foreign-owned firms. Very few services-producing establishments under investigation export substantial proportion of their services beyond the Klang Valley. While there are future possibilities, at present services-producing establishments do not show the ability to create urban economic impacts equal to or greater than manufacturing establishments. However, the present low exports may not necessarily be bad for Kuala Lumpur for money spent on inputs remains within the urban economy. Evidently, producer services production in Kuala Lumpur is still labour intensive to a certain extent but this again depend very much on the nature of services output.

Manufacturing industries still provide the central source of the growing demand for producer services in Kuala Lumpur. Proximity to the Multi Media Super Corridor (MSC) will undoubtedly benefit Kuala Lumpur in the long run with respect to the development of its producer services sector. The MSC is expected to accommodate worldwide cluster of high technology manufacturing activities. Apart from continued dependence on the manufacturing sector, there is some evident of the importance of other service providers and the construction industries as future sources of growth.

In Kuala Lumpur, the externalization dynamics of producer services development is clearly shown. The growth of producer services activities in terms of employment and output suggest that there has been a net growth in the supply of producer services over time, particularly between middle eighties and middle nineties. The net outcome of the dynamics of change concerning how producer services establishments meet the needs for these functions has been predominantly in favour of the local market. From the locational standpoint, these dynamics of change have been concentrated in Kuala Lumpur, in particular the central business district, including the Golden Triangle Area.

9.3. Policy Implications

After Singapore, Kuala Lumpur has a competitive advantage in the provision of producer services, in particular business services, in the South East Asian region. Kuala Lumpur should seek to maintain and even explore ways to extend such advantages. For business services and other upcoming information intensive services telecommunication infrastructures are of critical importance. Increased efficiency of producer services production is likely to have a significant impact on other productive sectors of the urban economy. A good example is the extent to which producer services could contribute to the effective production and distribution of manufactured goods. In the context of Kuala Lumpur in particular and Malaysia in general it is important for policy makers to think of the services-and goods-producing sectors in the economy as intertwined. Indeed, policy measures and mechanisms for one sector should be initiated and introduced with impacts on the other sector fully considered and assessed. Admittedly, services and manufacturing linkages and interactions cover a broad spectrum of activities in the urban economy. Many of these linkages remain to be explored and analyzed. Understanding of these will arguably determine the performance and competitiveness of not only manufacturing enterprises but also the services sector itself. Apart from the manufacturing sector, in an urban economy context, the interaction between services and the construction sector is another policy area to be given due emphasis.

From earlier discussion, weaknesses and gaps in government's strategies relating to export promotion are evident. The government to promote professional services overseas entrusts MATRADE. It has, before the economic meltdown, identified export constraints for Malaysian professional services firms such as their limited funds and manpower to seize opportunities overseas. They suffered from acute lack of information on various opportunities overseas. More importantly, these firms could not overcome restrictive and prohibitive rules and regulations and cost of doing business overseas. Limitations imposed by professional code of ethics made exportation of services very difficult. Realizing that economic difficulties in Malaysia made exportation of services very urgent MATRADE has embarked on a very challenging task to gather and disseminate information on opportunities abroad. It endeavors to expose and introduce local capabilities during missions/fairs, and advises and informs firms of export market conditions, requirements and procedures.

But a major impediment to exportation of professional services remains. Even though the Export and Import Bank of Malaysia (EXIM Bank), incorporated in 1995 and currently with authorized and paid-up capital of RM500 million and RM300 million respectively, is quite flexible in providing financing for the export of professional services through its export of services facility the approval process is very stringent. So far, only one computer firm has succeeded in getting this facility. The fact that export of services involves the movement of non-tangible entities made financing of export of services very difficult. Experiences of the establishments interviewed indicate areas where the government should concentrate on. Instead of placing the responsibility for export promotion solely in the hands of one agency, MATRADE, public agencies at all levels and the various professional services institutions should embark on promotional efforts complementing that of the central agency. However, the government should support first-time professional services providers at the export threshold or at the pre-engagement phase. On a more general level, the move towards multilateral rules on "Trade in Services" will eventually make trade arrangement more transparent, with it also the need to open up local markets. Logically, this can only mean that foreign suppliers will boldly seek out local markets supported by internal rules that are monitored by the

WTO. Arguably, unless Malaysian producer services firms are ready for competition not only will they loose out in the local market, they would also fail internationally.

Producer services have been shown to have certain locational needs, often only met in larger metropolitan areas. Within metropolitan areas, only selected locations are considered favourable by producer services activities. Producer services growth demands substantial infrastructure and continuous upgrading of this is crucial in order to enhance locational attractiveness. For this reason, attempts to create an effective producer service policy in non-metropolitan region may not be very successful.

The research findings reported in this book should generate some optimism among local policy makers as to the ability of producer services activities to stimulate urban economic growth. It has been shown that producer services are a very important component in the supply capacity of the urban economy. As such, there is scope for assistance to producer services sector as a means of generating employment growth either directly or indirectly. While recognizing the importance of producer services in the urban economy, it is important to realize that the heterogeneity that characterizes producer services activities means that the manner in which these activities are defined and aggregated may affect empirical claims above. This may inevitably impact upon policy recommendations.

9.4. Academic Contributions

The research findings so far provide insight into our knowledge and understanding of growth and development of producer services in an urban economy, which is increasingly integrated with the global economy. This study confirms the contention that producer services, at least in the context of Kuala Lumpur and other cities in the Asia Pacific region of similar complexity, provide coordinative support to the administrative units base. The expansion of the "loca"' manufacturing industry has generated greater demand for the local services sector and this adds substantially to the arguments with respect to the dominance of the "manufacturing-services linkage" and not "service-manufacturing linkage" or "service-service linkage". In other word, the postindustrial model of producer services growth and development whereby 'the development of this sector is directly tied to and predominantly dependent upon the resources generated by local service sector', as postulated in the theoretical framework was proven not quite true.

It is noteworthy that 'unbundling hypothesis' is predominantly responsible for producer services growth in Kuala Lumpur but then this tendency is triggered partly by the need to fulfil government requirements and regulations.

Some local producer services establishments have been able to maintain (prior to the 1997 economic and financial turmoil) their growth trajectory by increasing their trade with the non-local manufacturing industry. This finding fits quite easily into the various contentions on export or non-export capability of producer services establishments and the notion of the relationship between organizational characteristics if establishments and export movement.

9.5. Further Research

The research findings provide fresh insights into the growth and development of producer services activities in an urban economy that is rapidly expanding and experiencing structural transformation. Though the focus of the research has been upon the producer services sector in Kuala Lumpur, the underlying factors and processes may be relevant to other similar cities in this region.

In the process of this undertaking this study many more questions have arisen than have been answered. This highlights the need for other lines of enquiry that require attention if the process of producer services growth at the local level is to be fully understood. For example, it is useful to look at one particular sub-sector of the producer services category in greater detail. Appropriate candidates for case studies will be the information-intensive service sector or the logistics sub-sector such as air cargo industry.

The air cargo industry is of great interest. This industry is expected to benefit from the surge in electronic commerce as businesses increasingly turn to internet-based ordering, shipping and tracking options and drive up the demand for just-in-time delivery solutions. Businesses are also opting for cargo companies to manage their inventory and distribution systems with sophisticated software programmes. Increasingly, companies are reducing inventory levels by relying on integrators such as FedEx and others to ship products direct from factories to the ultimate customer without an intermediate stop in the seller's warehouse. Arguably, with advanced virtual warehousing solutions, sellers are able to manage this intricate delivery schedule and slash operating costs at the same time. While warehouses may not be totally eliminated the value of merchandise warehoused in the future would be drastically reduced. Dell Computer Corporation, for example, has been quoted as utilizing FedEx and United Parcel Service (UPS) to deliver materials first to parts assembly plants, then on to plants doing the final assembly of computer products and then on to customers. Interestingly, this allows buyers to receive custom-built computers that never spent time in a warehouse or on a retail store shelf but were almost always in motion. The economic benefits generated by the robust air cargo services goes beyond the fences of the airport. Arguably, the services injected substantial economic development into the community. For example, along with the expansion of the air cargo services concomitant development in intermodal system of shipping was noted. Trucking, for instance, is becoming a bigger part of the air cargo/air express business. Rapid expansion of air cargo has been a blessing for the aviation industry, as well as the companies that depend on e-commerce. Thus, new and interesting research areas relating to air cargo services in particular and transportation in general are becoming evident as a result of changes in global trade and advancement in technology.

REFERENCES

Aharoni, Y. ed. 1997. *Changing Roles of State Intervention in Services in an Era of Open International Markets*. Albany: State University of New York.

Ashton, D.J. and B.K. Sternal. 1978. *Business Services and New England's Export Base. Federal Reserve Bank of Boston*. Research Department Special Study.

Bagchi-Sen, S. and J. Sen. 1997. The Current State of Knowledge in International Business in Producer Services. *Environment and Planning A*. 29: 1153 - 1174.

Bank Negara Malaysia. 1996. *Annual Report, 1995*. Kuala Lumpur: Bank Negara Malaysia.

Bank Negara Malaysia. 1995. *Annual Report, 1994*. Kuala Lumpur: Bank Negara Malaysia.

Beyers, W.B. and D.P. Lindahl. 1996. Explaining the demand for Producer Services; Is Cost-driven Externalization the Major Factor? *Papers in Regional Science. The Journal of the RSAI*. 75, 3: 351-374.

Beyers, W.B. and M.J. Alvine. 1985. Export Services in Post-Industrial Society. *Papers of the Regional Science Association*. 57: 33-45.

Bloom, P. N. 1984. Effective Marketing for Professional Services. *Harvard Business Review*. 62, Sept.-Oct.: 102-110.

Browne, L. 1991. The Role of Services in New England's Rise and Fall: Engine of Growth or Along for a Ride. *New England Economic Review* (July/August): 27-44.

Browning, H.L. and J. Singelmann. 1975. *The Emergence of a Service Society: Demographic and Sociological Aspects of the Sectoral Transformation of the Labour Force in the U.S.A.* Springfield: V.A. National Technical Information Service.

Bryson, J. R. and P. W. Daniels. ed. 1998a. *Service Industries in the Global Economy. Volume 1. Service Theories and Service Employment.* Cheltenham: Edward Elgar Publishing Limited.

Bryson, J. R. and P. W. Daniels. ed. 1998b. *Service Industries in the Global Economy. Volume II. Services, Globalization and Economic Development.* Cheltenham: Edward Elgar Publishing Limited.

Buckley, M.J. and M. Casson. 1976. *The Future of Multinational Enterprise*. London: Macmillan.

Caves, R.E. 1971. International Corporations: the Industrial Economies of Foreign Investment. *Economica.* 38, Feb: 1-27.

Christopherson, S. and T. Noyelle. 1992. The U.S. Path Toward Flexibility and Productivity: The Re-Making of the U.S. Labour Market in the 1980's. In *Regional Development and Contemporary Industrial Respons,* edited by H. Ernste and V. Meier, 163-178. London: Belhaven Press.

Clark, C. 1951. Urban Population Densities. *Journal of the Royal Statistical Society, Ser. A.* 114: 490-6.

Clegg, J. 1993. Investigating the Determinants of Service Sector Foreign Direct Investment. In *The Growth of Global Business*, edited by H. Cox, J. Clegg, and G. Ietto-Gillies, 85-104. London: Routledge.

Code, W.R. 1983. The Strength of the Center: Downtown Offices and Metropolitan Decentralization Policy in Toronto. *Environment and Planning A.* 15: 1361-1380.

Coffey, W. 1992. The Role of Producer Services in Systems of Flexible Production. In *Regional Development and Contemporary Industrial Response*, edited by H. Ernste and V. Meier. 133-146. London: Belhaven Press.

Coffey, W.J. and A.S. Bailly. 1991. Producer Services and Flexible Production: An Exploratory Analysis. *Growth and Change*. 22, Fall: 95-117.

Coffey, W. and A.S. Bailly. 1992. Producer Services and Systems of Flexible Production. *Urban Studies*. 29: 857-868.

Coffey, W. and M. Polese. 1987a. Intrafirm Trade in Business Services: Implications for the Location of Office-based Services. *Paper of the Regional Service Association*. 62: 71-80.

Coffey, W. and M. Polese. 1987b. Trade and Location of Producer Services : A Canadian Perspective. *Environment and Planning, A*. 19: 597-611.

Coffey, W.J., Drolet, R. and M. Polese. 1996. The Intrametropolitan Location of High-Order Services: Patterns, Factors and Mobility in Montreal. *Papers in Regional Service. The Journal of the RSAI*. 75: 293-323.

Cox, K. R. 1995. Globalisation, Competition and the Politics of Local Development. *Urban Studies*. 32: 213-224.

Cox, H., Clegg, J. and G. Ietto-Gillies. 1993. *The Growth of Global Business*. London: Routledge.

Daniels, P.W. 1985. *Service Industries. A Geographical Appraisal.* London: Metheun.

Daniels, P.W. 1993. *Service Industries in the World Economy.* Oxford: Blackwell.

Daniels, P.W. 1998. Economic Development and Producer Services Growth : The APEC Experience. *Asia Pacific Viewpoint*. 39: 145-160.

Daniels, P. W., O' Connor, K., and T. A. Hutton. 1991. The Planning Response to Urban Service Sector Growth: an International Comparison. *Growth and Change*. 22, Fall: 3-26.

Davis, H.C. and T.A. Hutton. 1994. Marketing Vancouver's Services to the Asia Pacific. *The Canadian Geographer.* 38: 18-28.

Department of Statistics, Malaysia. 997. *Census of Professional and Institutional Establishment - Private Sector - 1994*. Kuala Lumpur: Department of Statistics.

Department of Statistics, Malaysia. 1994. *Census of Selected Service Industries, 1992*. Kuala Lumpur: Department of Statistics.

Department of Statistics, Malaysia. 1986. *Census of Selected Service Industries, 1984*. Kuala Lumpur: Department of Statistics.

Department of Statistics, Malaysia. 1986. *Census of Professional and Industrial Establishments - Private Sector - 1984*. Kuala Lumpur: Department of Statistics.

Dicken, P. 1992. *Global Shift: The Internationalization of Economic Activity*. New York: Guildford Press.

Drennan, M.P. 1992. Gateway Cities: The Metropolitan Sources of US Producer Services Exports. *Urban Studies*. 29: 127-235.

Dunning, J.H. 1988. Trade and Foreign-Owned Production in Services: Some Conceptual and Theoretical Issues. In *Services in World Economic Growth*, edited by H. Giersch. 108-150. Boulder, Co: Westview Press.

Dunning, J.H. 1977. Trade Location of Economic Activity and the Multinational Enterprise: A Search for an Electic Approach. In *The International Allocation of Economic Activity*, edited by B. Ohlin, O.O. Hesselborn, and P.M. Wijkman, Chapter 12. New York: Holmes and Meier.

Fuchs, V.R. 1968. *The Service Economy*. New York: National Bureau of Economic Research.

Gad, G. 1979. Face-to-face Linkages and Office Decentralization Potentials: A Study of Toronto. In *Spatial Patterns of Office Growth and Location*, edited by P. Daniels. 277-324. Chichester, UK: Willey.

Gad, G. 1985. Office Location Dynamics in Toronto: Suburbanization and Central District Specialization. *Urban Geography*. 6: 331-351.

Goe, W.R. 1990. Producer Services, Trade and the Social Division of Labour. *Regional Studies*. 24: 327-342.

Goe, W.R. 1991. The Growth of Producer Services Industries: Sorting through the Externalisation Debate. *Growth and Change*. 22: 118 - 41.

Goe, W.R. 1994. The Producer Services Sector and Development within the Deindustrializing Urban Community. *Social Forces*. 72, June: 971-1009.

Gottmann, J. 1977. Megalopolis and Antipolis: The Telephone and the Structure of the City. In *The Social Impact of the Telephone*, edited by I. de Sola Pool, 303-17. Cambridge, M.A.: MIT Press.

Government of Malaysia. 1996. *Seventh Malaysia Plan 1996-2000*. Kuala Lumpur: Percetakan Nasional Berhad.

Government of Malaysia. 1991. *Sixth Malaysia Plan 1991-1995*. Kuala Lumpur: Percetakan Nasional Berhad.

Greenfield, H. 1966. *Manpower and the Growth of Producer Services*. New York: Columbia University Press.

Grummesson, E. 1979. The Marketing of Professional Services: An Organisational Dilemma. *European Journal of Marketing*. 13: 308-18.

Hansen, N. 1991. Factories in Danish Fields: How High-Wage, Flexible Production has Succeeded in Peripheral Jutland. *International Regional Science Review*. 14: 109-132.

Hansen, N. 1990. Do Producer Services Induce Regional Economic Development? *Journal of Regional Science*. 30, 465-476.

Harrington, J. W. and H.S. Campbell. 1997. The Suburbanization of Producer Services Employment. *Growth and Change.* 28: 335-59.

Harrington, J.W. 1995. Producer Services Research in U.S. Regional Studies. *The Professional Geographer* . 47: 66-69.

Hatch, C. 1987. Learning from Italy's Industrial Renaissance. *The Entrepreneurial Economy*. 1: 4-11.

Hitchens, D.M.W.N., O'Farrell, P.N. and C.D. Conway. 1996. The Comparative Performance of Business Services in Northern Ireland and the Republic of Ireland. *Urban Studies*. 33, 7: 1110-1996.

Hutton, T.H. and D. Ley. 1987. Location Linkages and Labour: The Downtown Complex of Corporate Activities in a Medium Size City. Vancouver, British Columbia. *Economic Geography.* 63: 126-141.

Hymer, S.H. 1976. *The International Operations of National Firms: A Study of Direct Foreign Investment*. Cambridge MA.: MIT Press.

Julleff-Tranter, L.E. 1996. Advanced Producer Services: Just a Service to Manufacturing. *The Service Industries Journal.* 16, July: 389-400.

Katouzian, M.A. 1970. The Development of the Service Sector: A New Approach. *Oxford Economic Papers*. 22, Nov. : 362-382.

Kaynak, E. 1989. *Management of International Advertising: A handbook and guide for Professionals.* New York: Greenwood Press.

Keil, S. and R. Mack. 1986. Identifying Export Potentials in the Service Sector. *Growth and Change*. 17: 1-7.

Kindlebarger, C.P. 1969. *American Business Abroad: Six Essays on Direct Investment.* New Haven, CT: Yale University Press.

Leo, Pierre-Yves and J. Philippe. 1991. Multisited Versus Compact Producer Services Firms: Insights from the French Case. *Growth and Change*. 22: 142-156.

Ley, D. 1985. Downtown or Suburbs? A Comparative Study of Two Vancouver Head Offices. *Canadian Geographer.* 29: 30-43.

Lovelock, C. H. 1981. *Service Marketing*. New Jersey: Prentice Hall.

Marr, N. E. et al., 1996. Marketing and Professional Services: the Case of Consultancy Engineering. *The Service Industries Journal*. 16, Oct. : 544-562.

Marshall, J.W., Wood, P., Daniels, P.W., McKennon, A., Batchler, J., Danerick, P., Thrift, N., Gillespie, A., Green, A. and A. Leyshon. 1988. *Services and Uneven Development*. Oxford: Oxford University Press.

Marshall, N. and P. Wood. 1995. *Services and Space - Key Aspects of Urban and Regional Development*. Burnt Hill, Harlow: Longman Scientific and Technical.

Michalak, W.Z. and K.J. Fairbairn. 1993. The Location of Producer Services in Edmonton. *The Canadian Geographer*. 37: 2-16.

Miles, I. 1993. Services in the New Industrial Economy. *FUTURES.* July/August: 653-672.

Ministry of Finance Malaysia. 1985. *Economic Report 1985/86.* Kuala Lumpur: National Printing Department.

Ministry of Finance Malaysia. 1986. *Economic Report 1986/87*. Kuala Lumpur: National Printing Department.

Ministry of Finance Malaysia. 1987. *Economic Report 1987/88*. Kuala Lumpur: National Printing Department.

Ministry of Finance Malaysia. 1988. *Economic Report 1988/89*. Kuala Lumpur: National Printing Department.

Ministry of Finance Malaysia. 1989. *Economic Report 1989/90*. Kuala Lumpur: National Printing Department.

Ministry of Finance Malaysia. 1990. *Economic Report 1990/91*. Kuala Lumpur: National Printing Department.

Ministry of Finance Malaysia. 1991. *Economic Report 1991/92*. Kuala Lumpur: National Printing Department.

Ministry of Finance Malaysia. 1992. *Economic Report 1992/93*. Kuala Lumpur: National Printing Department.

Ministry of Finance Malaysia. 1993. *Economic Report 1993/94*. Kuala Lumpur: National Printing Department.

Ministry of Finance Malaysia. 1994. *Economic Report 1994/95*. Kuala Lumpur: National Printing Department.

Ministry of Finance Malaysia. 1995. *Economic Report 1995/96*. Kuala Lumpur: Percetakan Nasional Berhad.

Ministry of Finance Malaysia. 1996. *Economic Report 1996/97*. Kuala Lumpur: Percetakan Nasional Berhad.

Ministry of Finance Malaysia. 1997. *Economic Report 1997/98*. Kuala Lumpur: Percetakan Nasional Berhad.

Ministry of Finance Malaysia. 1998. *Economic Report 1998/99*. Kuala Lumpur: Percetakan Nasional Berhad.

Morshidi Sirat, 1998. Producer Services and Growth Management of a Metropolitan Region: The Case of Kuala Lumpur, Malaysia. *Asia Pacific Viewpoint*. 39, 2, August, 221-236.

Morshidi Sirat and Suriati Ghazali, 1999. *Globalisation of Economic Activity and Third World Cities: A Case Study of Kuala Lumpur*. Kuala Lumpur: Utusan Publications and Distributors.

Morshidi Sirat and Sharifah Rohaya Dawood, 2000. Issues of Small and Medium Scale Professional Service Firms. In *Small and Medium Enterprises in Asian Pacific Countries, Vol. 1 Roles and Issues*, edited by Moha Asri Abdullah and Mohd. Isa Bakar, 153-165. Huntington, NY: Nova Science Publishers, Inc.

Mountjoy, A.B. 1984. *Industrialization and Development Countries*. London: Hutchinson.

Noyelle, A. B. 1983. The Rise of Advanced Services. *American Planning Association Journal*. 49:280-90.

Noyelle, T. 1987. *Beyond Industrial Dualism: Market and Job Segmentation in the New Economy*. Boulder: Westview Press.

Noyelle, T.J. and T.M. Stanback. 1984. *The Economic Transformation of American Cities*. Totowa. N.J.: Rowman and Allanheld.

O'Connor, K. and T. A. Hutton. 1998. Producer Services in the Asia Pacific Region: An Overview of Research Issues. *Asia Pacific Viewpoint*. 39, Aug.: 139-143.

O'Connor, K. and D. Edington. 1991. Producer Services and Metropolitan Development in Australia. *Growth and Change*. 22:3-26.

O'Farrel, P. Moffat, L. and D. Hitchens. 1993. Manufacturing Demand for Business Services in a Core and Peripheral Region: Does Flexible Production Imply Vertical Dis-intergration of Business Service. *Regional Studies*. 27: 385-400.

O'Farrell, .N. and D.M.W.N. Hitchens.. 1988. Interfirm Comparisons in Industrial Research: The Utility of Matched Pairs Design. *Tjdschrift voor Economische en Sociale Geografie*. 79: 63-69.

O'hUallachain, B. and N. Reid. 1991. The Location and Growth of Business and Professional Services in American Metropolitan Areas. *Annals of the Association of American Geographers*. 13: 334-54.

Palmer, D., Friedland, R. Roussel, A. and P.D. Jennings. 1990. Corporations and the Urban Advanced Business Sector. *Social Forces*. 69: 115-137.

Perry, M. 1992. Flexible Production, Externalization and the Interpretation of Business Service Growth. *The Service Industries Journal*. 12: 1-16.

Perry, M. 1991. The Capacity of Producer Services to Generate Regional Growth: Some Evidence from a Peripheral Metropolitan Economy. *Environment and Planning, A*. 23: 1331-1347.

Persky, J. and W. Wiewel. 1994. The Growing Localness of the Global City. *Economic Geography*. April 1994: 129-143.

Porter, M. E. 1990. *The Competitive Advantage of Nation*. New York: The Free Press.

Porterfields, S .L. and G.C. Pulver. 1991. Exports, Imports, and Locations of Services Producers. *International Regional Science Review*. 14: 41-59.

Porterfield, S.L. and T.L. Cox. 1991. The Export Decision of Selected Services-Producing and Manufacturing Industries. *Growth and Change*. Summer, 22: 66-85.

Pred, A.R. 1975. Diffusion, Organizational Spatial Structure, and City System Development. *Economic Geography*. 51: 252-68.

Rugman, A.M. 1981. *Inside the Multinationals: The Economics of Internal Markets*. New York: Columbia University Press.

Sassen, S. 1991. *The Global City: New York, London, Tokyo*. Princeton, N.J.: Princeton University Press.

Schwartz, A. 1992. The Geograpy of Corporate Services: A Case Study of the New York Urban Region. *Urban Geography*. 13: 1-24.

Scott, A. 1988. *Metropolis. From Division of Labour to Urban Form*. Berkeley: University of California Press.

Sieh Lee Mei Ling, 1992. *Producer Services Development and Trade - Malaysia and ASEAN in the Uruguay Round*. Petaling Jaya: Producer Services Research Project and IDRC.

Sieh Lee Mei Ling, et al. 1995. *The Finance Company Industry of Malaysia : Current Status and Future Directions*. Kuala Lumpur: University Malaya Press.

Singelmann, J. 1978. *From Agriculture to Services: The Transformation of Industrial Employment*. Beverly Hills, CA: Sage.

Smith, S.M. 1984. Export-Orientation of Non-Manufacturing Businesses in Non-Metropolitan Communities. *American Journal of Agricultural Economic*. 66: 145-55.

Smith, S.M. and G.C. Pulver. 1981. Non-Manufacturing Businesses as a Growth Alternative in Non-Metropolitan Areas. *Journal of Community Development Society*. 12: 33-47.

Stabler, J.C. and E.C. Howe. 1988. Service Exports and Regional Growth in the Post-Industrial Era. *Journal of Regional Science*. 28: 303-316.

Stanback, T.M. Jr. 1979. *Understanding the Service Economy*. Baltimore, MD.: John Hopkins University Press.

Stanback, T.M. Jr., Bearse, P.J., Noyelle, T.J., and R.A. Karasek. 1981. *Services - The New Economy*. Totowa, N-J: Rowman & Allanheld.

Sulaiman, M and P.R. Nair. 1996. *Deficit in the Services Account of the Balance of Payment*. Kuala Lumpur: Malaysian Institute of Economic Research.

The STAR. 1997. 8 December.

Tornqvist, G.E., 1970. Contact Systems and Regional Development. University of Lund: *Lund Studies in Geography, Series B*. No. 38.

UNCTC (United Nations Centre on Transnational Corporations). 1988. *Transnational Corporations in World Development: Trends and Prospects*. United Nations - Centre on Transnational Corporations. New York: United Nations.

UNCTAD (United Nations Conference on Trade and Development). 1994. *Liberalizing International Transactions in Services - A Handbook*. New York and Geneva: United Nations.

United States Congress Office of Technology Assessment, 1987. *International Competition in Services*. Washington, DC. US.: Government Printing Office.

INDEX

A

account, 1, 15, 16, 20, 103, 115
accounting, 4, 5, 9, 27, 28, 36, 38, 50, 55, 66, 70, 76, 108, 109, 110, 111
activities, 2, 4, 5, 6, 7, 9, 10, 11, 14, 16, 23, 25, 26, 27, 28, 29, 31, 35, 36, 39, 40, 46, 49, 58, 63, 65, 66, 69, 70, 71, 73, 74, 75, 76, 82, 85, 91, 118, 121, 122, 125, 127, 128, 129, 130, 131, 132
advanced economies, 1
advertising, 5, 6, 9, 25, 28, 34, 49, 55, 58, 60, 63, 66, 70, 76, 81, 98, 100, 107, 112, 113, 114, 115, 116, 125, 128
agglomeration, 4, 70, 81
Aharoni, Y., 133
architecture, 76, 107
Asia Pacific, 1, 131, 134, 137, 138

B

balance of payment, 15, 20, 118
Bank Negara Malaysia, 15, 18, 133
banking, 9, 11, 122
Bloom, P. N., 133
Browne, L., 133

C

capital intensive, 76
Caves, R.E., 134
cities, 2, 4, 16, 46, 70, 131, 132
Clark, C., 134
classification, 9, 10
Clegg, J., 134
client-following, 5, 6
client-oriented, 5
Code, W.R., 134
commercial bank, 15
competition between cities, 1
competitive, 40, 86, 87, 89, 90, 93, 97, 100, 101, 103, 104, 108, 109, 111, 113, 114, 123, 128, 129
competitive advantage, 40, 86, 89, 93, 108, 111, 113, 129
competitive forces, 86
conceptual framework, 6, 7
consumption-oriented, 10
contact-rich, 5
corporate complex, 129
cost consideration, 3, 96, 111
cost leadership, 86, 88, 93
cost-driven, 2, 81, 95, 96

D

Daniels, P.W., 134, 136
definition, 9, 10, 12
delivery, 5, 12, 28, 81, 91, 132
demands, 3, 5, 6, 11, 16, 28, 40, 79, 97, 108, 122, 123, 131
Department of Statistics, Malaysia, 12, 51, 53, 54, 56, 57, 59, 61, 62, 134, 135
deregulation, 6, 16, 17, 90, 114
determinants of growth, 2
developing countries, 1, 93, 104, 127
development model, 83
Dicken, P., 135
differentiation, 81, 86, 87, 88, 93
Drennan, M.P., 135
Dunning, J.H., 135

E

economic, 1, 3, 4, 6, 7, 9, 10, 11, 14, 15, 16, 17, 40, 46, 69, 73, 74, 76, 79, 80, 82, 83, 85, 92, 103, 106, 107, 108, 109, 111, 115, 116, 117, 119, 123, 129, 130, 131, 132
economic crisis, 108, 109
economic sectors, 6, 14, 80
economic transformation, 46
economy, 2, 4, 7, 15, 16, 17, 20, 29, 31, 32, 46, 49, 69, 71, 75, 79, 82, 83, 114, 117, 122, 127, 129, 130, 131
employment, xi, 1, 4, 15, 20, 25, 26, 28, 32, 35, 36, 37, 46, 49, 50, 52, 54, 55, 61, 69, 71, 121, 127, 129, 131
endogenous, 7
engineering, 9, 26, 27, 36, 37, 76, 128
environment, 2, 5, 7, 11, 81, 86, 92, 95, 96, 97, 111, 113, 122
Europe, 1, 66
exogenous, 7
expenditure, 34, 35, 49, 50, 51, 52, 53, 54, 56, 58, 60
export, 3, 4, 10, 11, 28, 65, 73, 74, 75, 76, 79, 82, 83, 95, 103, 104, 105, 106, 107, 110, 115, 118, 121, 123, 124, 125, 127, 128, 129, 130, 131
export base, 3, 4, 76
export potential, 3, 79, 104, 115, 118, 123
export potentials, 3, 79, 115, 118, 123
export promotion, 103, 124, 130
exports, 4, 73, 123, 125, 129

F

face-to-face, 5, 11, 81
final, 6, 9, 10, 11, 12, 17, 49, 98, 121, 132
financial markets, 128
firm-specific, 5
fixed assets, xi, 49, 50, 55, 56, 58, 60, 62, 63
flexible production, 3
focus, 85, 86, 87, 88, 89, 90, 92, 93, 104, 132
focus strategy, 86, 87, 88, 90, 93
footloose, 40, 46
freight, 15
Fuchs, V.R., 135

G

global, 2, 16, 81, 108, 112, 114, 128, 129, 131, 132
globalization, 1, 7, 9, 16
globalizing cities, 127
goals, 85, 86, 91, 92, 93
Goe, W.R., 135
Golden Triangle Area, 46, 129
goods-oriented, 10
Gottmann, J., 135
Government of Malaysia, 19, 22, 23, 31, 135
Greenfield, H., 135
growth trajectory, 131
growth trend, 15

H

Hansen, N., 135, 136
Harrington, J.W., 136
Hatch, C., 136
hierarchy, 1, 4, 75, 128
high-order, 5, 46
Hymer, S.H., 136

I

imports, 15, 76
industrial model, 6
industrialization, 1, 9
industrializing, 5
industrially advanced, 5
industries, 10, 28, 32, 33, 34, 46, 103, 104, 113, 121, 125, 128, 129
information technology, 9, 109, 122
information-rich, 5
infostructure, 29, 113
in-house, 2, 83, 95, 96, 113
inputs, 3, 5, 14, 76, 79, 81, 83, 129
insurance, 1, 5, 9, 11, 14, 15, 17, 28, 31, 32, 40, 47, 70, 100
integration, 6, 95, 119
intermediate, 5, 9, 10, 14, 17, 20, 28, 132
intermetropolitan, 3
internalization, 5, 6
internationalization, 4, 5, 6
interurban, 3, 5
interurban location, 5
interurban mobility, 5

J

Julleff-Tranter, L.E., 136

K

Katouzian, M.A., 136
Kaynak, E., 136
Klang Valley, 70, 73, 74, 75, 79, 82, 112, 116, 128, 129

knowledge workers, 120, 121
knowledge-based, 9
Kuala Lumpur, vi, ix, xi, xii, xiii, 6, 7, 11, 13, 16, 18, 29, 31, 32, 33, 34, 35, 36, 37, 38, 39, 40, 41, 42, 43, 44, 45, 46, 49, 50, 51, 52, 53, 54, 55, 56, 57, 58, 59, 60, 61, 62, 63, 65, 66, 67, 69, 70, 71, 73, 74, 75, 79, 82, 83, 99, 102, 107, 108, 112, 119, 123, 127, 128, 129, 131, 132, 133, 134, 135, 136, 137, 138, 139

L

Ley, D., 136
locational tendencies, 40, 46
location-specific, 5, 6
Lovelock, C. H., 136

M

Malaysia, xi, xii, xiii, 6, 7, 11, 12, 15, 18, 19, 20, 22, 23, 24, 25, 26, 27, 28, 29, 31, 32, 33, 34, 35, 36, 37, 38, 39, 51, 53, 54, 56, 57, 59, 61, 62, 65, 74, 75, 76, 81, 82, 87, 95, 104, 105, 106, 107, 108, 110, 111, 113, 114, 115, 116, 118, 119, 120, 121, 123, 124, 125, 127, 128, 130, 133, 134, 135, 136, 137, 138
Malaysia Technology Development Corporation (MTDC), 119
marketing, 4, 28, 66, 75, 76, 81, 83, 105, 106, 107, 111, 112, 116, 117, 118, 121, 124, 125
markets, 1, 3, 4, 6, 11, 29, 40, 65, 66, 74, 75, 79, 81, 82, 86, 87, 88, 89, 98, 100, 103, 104, 105, 108, 110, 113, 114, 117, 118, 121, 123, 124, 125, 128, 130
market-seeking, 6
metropolitan, 1, 4, 29, 47, 70, 73, 74, 75, 82, 83, 127, 131
Metropolitan Area, 138
metropolitan areas, 1, 4, 29, 131
Miles, I., 136
mobility, 66, 70
monopolistic, 6
Multi-Media Super Corridor, 29, 119
multinational, 6, 108, 128
multiplier, 4
multi-site, 65, 70, 74, 108

N

non-cost consideration, 2
non-local, 68, 73, 74, 81, 83, 129, 131
non-spatial, 7
North America, 1, 70
Noyelle, T., 137, 139

O

oliogopolistic, 6
open markets, 109
organization, 2, 11, 46, 66, 77, 85, 86, 91, 92, 109, 113, 116, 128
organizational changes, 2
organizational structures, 65
output, 75, 129
outsourcing, 3
ownership, xi, 6, 50, 51, 53, 54, 55, 56, 57, 58, 59, 60, 61, 62, 68, 73, 76, 80, 83, 101, 102, 128
ownership-specific, 5, 6

P

perceptions, 95, 107, 123
Perry, M., 138
Persky, J. and W. Wiewel, 138
personal services, 9
policies, 7, 11, 28, 29, 90, 98, 101, 103
policy implications, 46, 127
Porter, M. E., 138
producer services, 1, 2, 3, 4, 5, 6, 7, 9, 10, 11, 12, 14, 15, 16, 17, 28, 29, 31, 40, 46, 49, 63, 65, 69, 70, 71, 73, 74, 75, 76, 79, 80, 81, 82, 83, 85, 87, 95, 96, 97, 103, 104, 106, 107, 111, 118, 123, 127, 128, 129, 131, 132
professional, 9, 11, 12, 14, 16, 20, 25, 26, 27, 28, 35, 36, 37, 38, 70, 75, 98, 100, 101, 102, 104, 110, 111, 113, 119, 124, 125, 128, 130
promotional activities, 11
pure-cost, 2

R

regulations, 3, 81, 96, 97, 98, 100, 101, 102, 103, 109, 110, 111, 114, 118, 128, 130, 131
reorganization, 6
revenue, xi, 49, 50, 52, 53, 55, 58, 59, 60, 63, 75, 79, 80, 82, 112
rise and growth, 2
role and contribution, 1, 2, 65, 127

S

salaries, 49, 50, 52, 60, 63, 116
sales, 3, 73, 74, 75, 76, 79, 80, 83
Sassen, S., 138
Schwartz. A.. 138

Scott, A., 138
service sector, 2, 4, 5, 6, 9, 10, 14, 28, 32, 46, 49, 80, 83, 127, 128, 131, 132
services-producing, 129
Seventh Malaysia Plan, 22, 28, 135
share of employment, 4, 17, 20
Sieh Lee Mei Ling, 138
Singelmann, J., 138
single-site, 65, 66, 70, 71, 74
skills, xiii, 3, 28, 96, 97, 114, 115
Smith, S.M., 139
social, 9, 11, 46, 129
spatial, 7, 29, 46, 66, 81, 128, 129
specialization, 4
specialize, 88, 89
Stanback, T.M. Jr., 139
STAR, The, 16, 139
strategies, 5, 7, 11, 28, 46, 83, 85, 86, 88, 93, 117, 118, 124, 125, 130
strategy, 3, 11, 28, 40, 66, 85, 86, 87, 88, 90, 93, 106, 107, 108, 109, 110, 117, 124
subcontracting, 2

T

technological content, 9
telecommunication, 76, 99, 112, 115, 121, 129
temporal, 7
tertiary services, 9
Tornqvist, G.E., 139
tourism, 15, 20, 28
trade, 3, 4, 9, 17, 18, 31, 65, 73, 74, 75, 80, 82, 83, 105, 106, 107, 116, 117, 118, 124, 125, 127, 129, 130, 131, 132
transaction cost, 3
transformative industries, 10
transnational, 7, 16

U

unbundling hypothesis, 131
UNCTAD, 9, 139
UNCTC, 5, 139
United States Congress Office of Technology Assessment, 9, 139
urban, 1, 3, 4, 6, 7, 11, 14, 40, 46, 65, 66, 69, 73, 74, 75, 82, 83, 107, 127, 128, 129, 130, 131, 132
urban areas, 1, 4, 82
urban economy, 3, 4, 6, 7, 11, 46, 66, 107, 127, 129, 130, 131, 132
utilization, 3, 85, 89, 93

V

value-chain, 28

W

WTO, 131